AF576533

SITES UNSEEN

For Cynthia—
With Best Regards—
Shimon Attie 1999

SITES UNSEEN

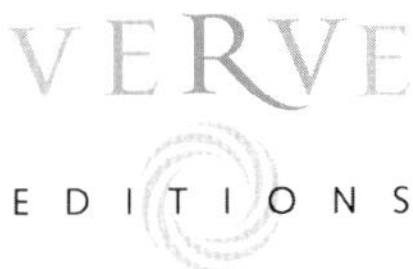

431 Pine Street, Burlington, VT 05401
email: verve@together.net

Library of Congress Cataloging-in-Publication Data
Attie, Shimon, 1957
Sites Unseen/Shimon Attie, Introduction by James Young
ISBN 0-9660352-1-6 (cloth)
1. Photography, Artistic, 2. Installation (Art)
3. Jews in art, 4. Jews-Pictorial works
779/.994
DS135.G4 1998

Published in 1998
by Verve Editions, Ltd. Burlington, Vermont

Designed and produced by Blank & Reschke,
Berlin, Germany
Printed and bound by Longo Frangart,
Bozen, Italy

All photographs by Shimon Attie with exception
of page number 21, courtesy of BizArt,
Copenhagen and Bent Ryberg.

SITES UNSEEN

SHIMON ATTIE **EUROPEAN PROJECTS**

INSTALLATIONS AND PHOTOGRAPHS

WITH AN INTRODUCTION BY JAMES YOUNG

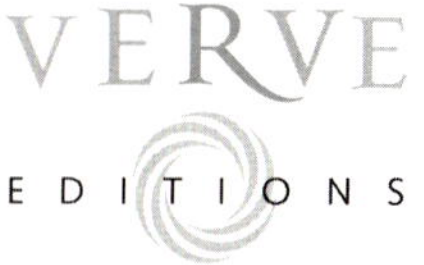

ACKNOWLEDGEMENTS

I am deeply indebted to the many individuals and organizations who helped make this book and the last 5 years of my work possible.

I am first and foremost thankful to my friend and colleague, Mathias Maile, who encouraged me early on when we first discussed the possibility of realizing a series of projects across the European continent. My projects in Dresden, Copenhagen and Cologne were full collaborative works between Mathias and myself, and I will always be grateful for his extraordinary artistic and technical talents. I would also like to thank Karlheinz Reimann, who was responsible for the technical realization of my projects in Amsterdam and Krakow.

I would like to thank Lars Moller and Jesper Soholm of BizArt, Copenhagen, who produced and organized *Portraits of Exile*, as well as Loa Bendix who served as the project manager. Lars and Jesper worked extremely hard to make the project a reality. Loa did an excellent job coordinating the many individuals and logistics involved in realizing such a large and ambitious project.

Udo Kittelmann, the director of the Cologne Kunstverein, organized *Brick by Brick*, and was instrumental in getting permission from *Art Cologne* to do this project. His enthusiastic support was indispensable in shepherding the project through the proper channels in Cologne. Dr. Barbara Jaeckli, at the Documentation Center for National Socialism, was extremely helpful in providing archival images and historical materials related to the history of the Cologne Fair Building.

Bas Vroege, director of the Paradox Foundation in the Netherlands, organized and produced *The Neighbor Next Door*. Bas's endless energy, enthusiasm and advocacy made the project possible. Deanna Herst, the project manager, worked tirelessly to ensure the success of *The Neighbor Next Door*, as did Marieke Istha, the project assistant. The Dutch Photo Archives in Rotterdam and the Film Archive of the Netherlands Government Information Service in The Hague were both generous in allowing film footage and other materials from their archives to be used for the project.

Heinz Jurgens, director of the Goethe Institute, and Dr. Joachim Russek, director of the Center for Jewish Culture-Judaica Foundation, both located in Krakow, were instrumental in organizing and providing funding for *The Walk of Fame*. Heinz and Joachim were invaluably open and flexible as the concept for the project evolved and changed. Robert Gadek, at the Center for Jewish Culture-Judaica Foundation, was of great help in coordinating many of the project's logistical needs, and also provided warm hospitality.

Tanja Hoffmann and Mathias Fisher gave generously of their time and effort in organizing the first exhibition of my Berlin project, *The Writing on the Wall*, in the Galerie im *Scheunenviertel*. Dr. Hermann Simon of the New Synagogue Foundation was instrumental in organizing financial support for the project early on, as was Dr. Rolf Bothe, former director of the Berlin Museum. Eike Geisel was more than generous in giving me unlimited access to his personal photographic archives, as well as providing encouragement and support in the initial stages of the project.

I am deeply indebted to the small Jewish community of Dresden, whose members loaned me photographs and images from family photograph albums so that I could realize *Trains*. Mr. Aris of the Jewish community was particularly helpful in organizing this effort. The Deutsches Hygiene Museum in Dresden was invaluable in organizing and providing logistical support for the project.

When large-scale public art projects are realized, there are often dozens of individuals who help behind the scenes with the installation, often simply because they believe in the work. To these individuals, too numerous to mention here by name, I offer my heartfelt thanks for your energy and generosity. My work would not have been possible without you.

I am grateful to my friends Axel Huhn and Ori Levy for providing me with a wealth of support while I worked on these projects, but especially for being my family in Berlin. Ruth and Marsha Attie's help in managing my affairs while I was realizing these projects allowed me to more fully concentrate on the completion of my work.

I deeply appreciate having had the experience of working with Kai Reschke, the book's designer. Kai helped greatly with his ideas and suggestions throughout all stages of conceiving and designing this book. Lothar Steffens and Johannes Nowak showed great patience and talent in printing the color reproductions in this volume.

Margo Perin was extremely helpful in editing my text for this book. Günter Braus, my publisher, has always been an enthusiastic supporter of my work, and helped in every way he could, from making an introduction for me with German television to taking on the financial risk of *Sites Unseen.* I would like to thank and acknowledge those institutions whose funding made my projects possible:

Portraits of Exile, Copenhagen, Denmark
The Danish Ministry of Culture's Cultural Fund, Copenhagen
The Danish Ministry of Interior, Copenhagen
The Kaleidescope program of the European Union (Europe-wide cultural sponsoring program), Brussels
The National Bank of Denmark's Anniversary Foundation of 1968, Copenhagen
The City of Copenhagen Cultural Fund
The Goethe Institute, Copenhagen
The Queen Ingrid and King Frederik's Fund, Copenhagen
BizArt, Copenhagen

Brick by Brick, Cologne, Germany
The Kaleidescope program of the European Union, Brussels

The Neighbor Next Door, Amsterdam, Netherlands
The Mondriaan Foundation, Amsterdam
The Gijselaar-Hintzen Foundation, Haarlem
The Kaleidescope program of the European Union, Brussels

The Walk of Fame, Krakow, Poland
The Goethe Institute, Krakow
The Center of Jewish Culture-Judaica Foundation, Krakow

The Writing on the Wall, Berlin, Germany
The New Synagogue Foundation, Berlin
The Berlin Museum, Berlin

Trains, Dresden, Germany
The Saxony Cultural Foundation, Dresden
The City of Dresden Cultural Ministry
The Saxonian Newspaper (*Sächsische Zeitung*), Dresden

I would also like to acknowledge those companies which provided sponsorship through donations of materials, labor, and discounts:
Siemens Company, Copenhagen
M8 Visual Design, Berlin
Capi-Lux Vak, Amsterdam
Tela Film, Amsterdam

Additionally, I would like to thank the public authorities, organizations and business establishments which gave permission for my projects to be realized on their property and premises:
The Copenhagen Harbor Authority
German Railway, Dresden
I & O Computer Services, Amsterdam
G. G. Special Sizes clothing store, Amsterdam
Degenaar Art Gallery, Amsterdam
ArtCologne, the Association of German Art Galleries, and the Cologne Fair and Exhibition Corporation
The Jewish Museum and Old Synagogue, Krakow

Lastly, I gratefully acknowledge the generous visual artist fellowships I received from the following institutions which supported me while I realized these projects:
The National Endowment for the Arts, Washington, D.C.
Art Fund (Kunstfonds), Bonn
The Cultural Fund Foundation (Stiftung Kulturfonds), Berlin
The Berlin Ministry of Culture (Der Senator für Kultur, Berlin)
The Memorial Foundation for Jewish Culture, New York
Art Matters, Inc., New York

Shimon Attie

CONTENTS

FOREWORD

The artworks of Shimon Attie are like gymnastic leaps of faith. First, they require a move backward in time to individual lives and to places that historical events have erased and destroyed. Then, Attie's art – projections of light that float seamlessly on architectural facades, or rise hauntingly from underwater, or announce themselves blatantly on street lamps and telephone poles – demands another leap. This time the movement is forward to the present, where images from the past are joined to the current moment. The works tug on buried memories. They conjure up frozen images from first hand experience or from knowledge gained from books, newspapers and magazines. And in that dissonance – the erased resurrected in the present – lies the power and the punch of Shimon Attie.

The movies are full of "magic moments" where editing makes the impossible seem real, even though we know that what we see could not possibly happen. Attie's projections, using the same tools of camera and light, editing and juxtaposition, also create these moments of suspended disbelief. His work is spectral both in its conjuring of uneasy ghosts from the past as well as in the artist's manipulation of the photographic tools.

Sites Unseen is a rare opportunity to see the photographs of Attie's European projections and installations, and to sense the power they had as events *in situ*. It is also an opportunity to understand the photographs as aesthetic objects that employ frame, cropping, saturation, perspective, and composition in ways our human eyes do not register. The intense purple of the sky in the projection of the Biograph Theatre, Berlin's first movie theatre, may have been lost to the passerby amazed to chance upon it in the city streets. But the encounter with Attie's photographs on the walls of a museum, gallery, or home is a deliberate, focused, and controlled experience of equal, though not random force. This publication documents both the events and the photographs, using the vocabulary of multiple generations to preserve and transmit a deeply felt sense of history, presence, and passage.

In Amsterdam, Berlin, Krakow, Copenhagen, Dresden, and soon in New York, San Francisco, and Boston, Shimon Attie makes art from the simple act of remembering and makes remembering the subject of art. The German émigré philosopher Theodor Adorno, in writing on the idea of tradition, commented, "A question doesn't exist that could be asked in which knowledge of the past is not kept, and which doesn't press on ahead to the future." In Shimon Attie's remembrances and references to a past he did not experience first hand, he is neither romantic nor nostalgic. Instead, the beautiful, haunting art of Shimon Attie is one of compression and expansion, propelling us backwards and forwards in both jarring and graceful leaps of memory and imagination.

Jill S. Medvedow, Director
The Institute of Contemporary Art, Boston
May 1998

PREFACE

Like all artists, I resist being "ghettoized." I am neither a politician nor a historian, nor do I claim to speak to anyone from a higher moral ground. Rather, my language is primarily a visual and aesthetic one. I am most interested in the relationship between place, memory, and identity and how this relationship might be distilled and expressed through visual and aesthetic means.

Together with selected images from *The Writing on the Wall* project which have been reintroduced in the last chapter of this book, this volume represents almost five years of my work. Although each project is unique and intended to stand on its own, together they represent a body of work in which the viewer can trace the direction my artwork has taken over the last several years.

Following the completion of *The Writing on the Wall* project in Berlin's *Scheunenviertel* neighborhood in early 1993, I decided to work in other European cities. I wanted to reflect, through installation art and photography, each city's history (both actual and mythologized), physical landscape, and present day social and political realities. I was specifically interested in exploring how each of these cities reconstructs its shared legacy of the Second World War and how each, in light of this legacy, responds to the present-day Europe-wide challenges of immigration, refugees (both economic and political), and the rise of ultra-nationalism and ethnic intolerance. This led me to conceive and realize the series of projects across the European continent, from Amsterdam and Cologne, to Copenhagen, Dresden, and Krakow, which comprise this book.

I came to these cities and cultures not as a *tabula rasa* or "objective observer," but as an artist profoundly influenced by the stories about the war told to me as a small child by my parents and their friends, some of whom were Holocaust survivors. I learned through these stories, particularly those told by my father, that part of being Jewish meant I was connected to a life and culture that no longer existed. This feeling, of having lost something I had never had, akin to that one might have for a grandparent who passed away before one's birth, was a powerful thread running through my childhood and has deeply influenced my work.

I photograph the installations myself because I believe the documentation of my projects is an integral part of the artistry. The photographs are not intended to merely record the installations; rather, through conscious composition and framing, their purpose is to point to the larger relationship between the installation and the environment in which it takes place.

While the projects themselves are long gone, I intend for the images in this book to have a life and power of their own.

Shimon Attie
1997

JAMES E. YOUNG

SITES UNSEEN: SHIMON ATTIE'S ACTS OF REMEMBRANCE 1991–1996

Some people claim intuitively to sense the invisible aura of past events in historical sites, as if the molecules of such sites still vibrated with the memory of their past. Shimon Attie is not so naive. He knows that this presence of the past is apparent only to those already familiar with a site's history, or to those who actually carry a visual memory of this site from another, earlier time. For Attie, memory of a site's past does not emanate from within a place but is more likely the projection of the mind's eye onto a given site. Without the historical consciousness of visitors, these sites remain essentially indifferent to their pasts, altogether amnesiac. They "know" only what we know, remember only what we remember.

For by themselves, these sites lack what Pierre Nora has called "the will to remember." That is, without a deliberate act of remembrance, buildings, streets, or ruins remain little more than inert pieces of the cityscape. Without the will to remember, Nora suggests, the place of memory "created in the play of memory and history … becomes indistinguishable from the place of history."[1] If it is true that such places of memory exist "only because of their capacity for metamorphosis," as Nora believes, then here we will examine the work of an artist as agent of metamorphosis, one whose acts of remembrance transform the sites of history into the sites of memory.

In *Sites Unseen*, Shimon Attie's series of European installations between 1991 and 1996, the artist has not only projected his necessarily mediated memory of a now lost Jewish past onto otherwise forgetful sites. But in so doing, he has also attempted a simultaneous critique of his own hyper-mediated relationship to the past. By literally bathing the sites of a now invisible Jewish past in the photographic images of their historical pasts, he simultaneously looks outward and inward for memory: for he hopes that once seen, the images of these projections will always haunt these sites by haunting those who have seen his projections. The sites of a lost Jewish past in Europe would thus retain traces of this past, if now only in the eyes of those who have seen Attie's installations.

When Shimon Attie moved to Berlin in 1991, he found a city haunted by the absence of its murdered and deported Jews. Like many Jewish Americans preoccupied by the Holocaust and steeped in its seemingly ubiquitous images, he saw Jewish ghosts in Europe's every nook and cranny: from the *Scheunenviertel* in Berlin to the central train station in Dresden; from the canals of Copenhagen to those of Amsterdam; from Cologne's annual art fair to Krakow's Kazimierz neighborhood. For Attie, however, private acts of remembrance in which he alone saw the faces and forms of now absent Jews in their former neighborhoods were not enough. He chose, therefore, to actualize these inner visions, to externalize them, and in so doing to make them part of a larger Public's memory. Once thus actualized, he hoped, these images would continue to haunt the sites even when no longer visible, that they would enter the inner worlds of all who saw them. He hoped that once others had become witnesses to his memorial projections, the installations themselves would no longer be necessary.

At the same time, *Sites Unseen* was not intended as a series of simple recollective acts, attempts to repair a broken past-continuous. Each installation also recast memory in some way, remarking its own relationship to the site even as it explored the site's relationship to its past. As a result, each of these projects sustained a certain, yet subtle ambivalence toward itself, even as each mixed the kinds of memory it generated. At each stage, the distance from personal to public memory was measured, as well as the reciprocal exchange between a specific site and its national context, the ways every site resonates with a nation's self-idealizations.

Part photography, part installation, and part performance, the totality of these projects might best be described as "acts of remembrance" – retaining the resonance of actions, staged acts, actors, and acting out. For in equal measure, they included the literal actions that brought them into being, created actors of local residents, staged interactions between local residents and their homes, provided a medium for the artist's own acting out of his obsession with the void left by Europe's absent Jews. Nor should this present volume be mistaken for the "acts of remembrance" it documents, which like the historical events being commemorated, are now over. Rather, this book is an after-image in its own right, a reflection on these acts.

In the pages that follow, therefore, I ask what happens between the mind of someone like Attie, saturated in the public iconography of the Holocaust, and the actual sites of history now seemingly oblivious to their pasts. On the one hand, Attie the artist is painfully aware that all he knows and remembers of the Holocaust has been passed down to him by others – shaped and filtered by a nation's self-aggrandizing myths, by a popular culture more intent on entertaining than teaching him. Moreover, he knows that his art-work will inevitably interpose yet another stratum of mediation between history and memory, another layer of images that might be confused for the history they would recall.

But then, Attie has no alternative. Instead of memory-acts that collapse the distinction between themselves and the past, therefore, he proposes acts of remembrance that expose just this gulf between what happened in the past and how it now gets remembered. Whether it is national myth and self-idealization or the silver-screen and its compelling artifice that blurs the distinction between actual past and present memory of it, or whether it is only the muteness of a cityscape that hides its history, Attie makes as his object of memory the distance between then and now, the ways that even his own acts of remembrance cannot but gesture indirectly to what was lost and how we now recall it.

I. The Writing on the Wall: Berlin, 1991–1993

"After finishing art school in San Francisco, I came to Berlin in the summer of 1991," Shimon Attie writes in his introduction to a book for *The Writing on the Wall.* "Walking the streets of the city that summer, I felt myself asking over and over again, Where are all the missing people? What has become of the Jewish culture and community which had once been at home here? I felt the presence of this lost community very strongly, even though so few visible traces of it remained."[2] Strangely enough, it was not the absence of Berlin's lost Jews that Attie felt so strongly, but their presence. For in fact, though they may have been invisible to others walking those same streets, Attie's memory and imagination had already begun to repopulate the *Scheunenviertel* district in Berlin with the Jews of his mind.

After several weeks of photographic research in Berlin's archives, Attie had found dozens of images from the *Scheunenviertel* of the 1920's and 1930's and was able to pinpoint nearly one-quarter of their precise locations in the current neighborhood just east of Berlin's Alexanderplatz, formerly in the eastern sector of the city. That September, only three months after moving to Berlin, Attie began projecting slides of these photographs onto the same or nearby addresses where they had been taken earlier in the century. "*The Writing on the Wall* grew out of my response to the discrepancy between what I felt and what I did not see," Attie explains. "I wanted to give this invisible past a voice, to bring it to light, if only for some brief moments." And so for the next year, weather permitting, Attie projected these images of Jewish life from the *Scheunenviertel* before the Holocaust back into present-day Berlin. Each installation ran for one or two evenings, visible to local residents, street traffic and passersby. During these projections, the artist also photographed the installations themselves in time exposures lasting from three to four minutes. The resulting photographs of the installations have been exhibited widely in galleries and museums, works of fine art in their own right, and collected in the present volume.

But in fact, the artist is all too aware of the difference between the public installations *in situ* and their own reduced and codified standing in a gallery or catalogue. "The point was to intervene in a public space and project right onto those spaces," he has said. "One can always overlay images in a darkroom or with a computer. But I wanted to touch those spaces." Or one might add, he wanted to "re-touch" those spaces the way one re-touches photographs. For the photographic process – in literal and metaphorical ways – lies at the heart of this project: as the original archival photographs captured traces of reflected light and dark from the pre-war *Scheunenviertel*, the artist's photographs of the installations would now capture the light of the photographic images themselves as projected onto building walls. The analogue between the mechanical process of photography and the memory of images recorded by the mind's eye is literalized here: in both cases, reflected light imprints itself on light-sensitive surfaces, whether film or retina, that bear its traces afterwards.

For Attie recognizes at the outset that public spaces, even the dreariest in our day-to-day lives, also reflect meaning and significance back to us. They also become "art" in the eyes of beholders, at once framed and composed by our reflective gaze. Obversely, the projections themselves also served as inside-out "-frames" for all that surrounds them, turning the rock-hard reality of the present into an extension of the past images now embedded in it.

Once projected onto the peeling and mottled building facades of this quarter, these archival images seem less the reflections of light than illuminations of figures emerging from the shadows. From the doorways, in particular, former Jewish residents seem to be stepping out of a third dimension. Some, like the resident standing in the doorway at Joachimstraße 2, are caught unaware by both the original photographer and now, it seems, by us. Others, like the religious book salesman at the corner of what was formerly the corner of Grenadierstraße and Schendelgasse, seems to have been interrupted by the photographer, and has turned his head sideways to gaze impassively back at us. Because the streets of the delapidated *Scheunenviertel* (called the *Finstere Medine*, or "dark quarter" by its Yiddish speaking denizens) are still largely run down, as were many parts of the formerly East Berlin when the wall came down, the projected images added a life to these streets that they appeared otherwise not to have.

If the projected images of Jews going in and out of buildings, or sitting in windows, or huddled on a corner suggest themselves as a material part of the space they now reinhabited, once photographed, the subjects in these installations take on formal qualities not so apparent in the installations. As works now independent of the installations they represent, the photographs also recompose them, highlighting not only the apparition of a spatial, human dimension created in the installation but also now the iconographic play of signs and symbols. The Hebrew lettering of Yiddish signs mixes with German gothic lettering in the images, both now strewn together anarchically with painted post-wall graffiti – all of it a kind of literary detritus on scarred walls. The projected lettering of Meier Silberberg's kosher butcher shop at Mulackstraße 37 runs into the taggings of graffiti artists and post-unification slogans like "The struggle continues." Even more dramatic in its silence is the photograph of a slide-installation from the corner of Joachimstraße and Auguststraße: the barely visible head of a Jew in prayer philacteries beneath a white Star of David beams over the doorway of a dark building, itself backlighted by the rosy pink of a sunset. The star stands in stark, formally eloquent contrast to three rows of crucifix-like white window-panes on the dark building across the street, arrayed like a battle formation of crusader shields.

Even the human figures of Jews, animated by the play of light and air on textured surfaces, are reformalized in the photographs of the installations, hardened once again into the icons of "*Ost-Juden.*" It was the traditionally-garbed Jews of Eastern Europe, after all, who had moved into this quarter in the 1910's and 1920's, already a netherworld of criminals, prostitutes and the dispossessed. But it is not this unlikely mixture of the sacred and profane that Attie hopes to capture here. Rather it is a type, "the Jew" of the Germans' minds so long associated with long black caftans, beards and earlocks that Attie brings back to haunt current residents. Because German Jewry itself was often so well assimilated as to appear effectively invisible, Attie has had to rely on the image of *Ost-Juden* to make visible the otherwise invisible Jews of Germany – even though they themselves were not representative faces of German-Jewry itself.

In this way, these installations were also a somewhat literal metaphor for projecting his own inner desires onto the walls around him. All of us wish we could bring the victims back to life, to repair the terrible wound. But *The Writing on the Wall* is no such reparation or bringing back to life; it is, rather, the reminder of what was *lost*, not what was. At the same time, it is clear in Attie's mind, as he means for it be in ours, that these projections are simulations, not historical reconstructions. Their immense value lies not in showing us literally what was lost but in showing that loss itself is part of this neighborhood's history, an invisible but essential feature of its landscape.

II. Trains: Dresden, 1993

Unlike the *Scheunenviertel* in Berlin haunted by its now absent Jews, the Dresden train station seemed to Attie haunted by its absence of any sign of the central role train stations played throughout Germany during the Holocaust. These were the sites of collections for deportations, the last places many German Jews ever saw of their homeland, the tracks constituting a literal, material line connecting Germany to the death camps. In keeping with his medium of photographic projections, Attie and his collaborator, Mathias Maile, found photographs of Dresden's former Jewish citizens who had either been deported or who had emigrated and then projected them back into the city's central railway station.

In many ways, this project was more confrontational than *The Writing on the Wall*, which had more passively chastened local citizens for letting their former neighbors disappear into the ether of time. For in projecting specific faces from Dresden's Jewish community directly onto the trains, tracks and walls of the central station, Attie and Maile linked the photographic memory of the victims directly to their fate. Train stations were, after all, the literal sites of deportation, of emigration, of German-Jewish leavetaking. After culling some dozen images from family albums of Dresden's tiny Jewish community, Attie converted them into high-contrast black and white slides. For two weeks beginning on the 9th of November 1993 (the anniversary of *Kristallnacht*), images of handsome, smartly dressed young and middle-aged men and women shone brightly from the rafters of the station; other images of sad-eyed Jews peered up at travellers from the tracks, or stared down rebukingly from the walls, or confronted travellers face to face from the sides of trains. The daily, familiar routine of travel would be estranged and disrupted by these immense black and white projections; weekend holidays would have to commence on a decidely melancholy, less festive note. For a few moments every day, post-war Germans would be haunted by the vicarious memory of an American Jew. Now they, too, would be forced to see and remember what the Jewish traveller cannot put out of his mind: that on this platform, on these tracks, the Jews whose faces I see began to die.

In a similar installation in Hamburg, Attie had initially projected such images without the benefit of explaining captions. But when a curious passerby asked him, whether these were the pictures of the German Railway founders, he decided to mount large posters that made the source of these images explicitly clear. With this lesson in mind, he repeated the process in Dresden. He had wanted the rebuke of memory to come from within as the significance of these images dawned on travellers – now trapped in this conflation of time and space. The more he had to explain, he felt, the less successful and more coercively didactic the project became. But as word of the memorial projections spread, his accompanying captions became less necessary; and in the end, as tens of thousands of travellers saw and thereby internalized these images, the projections themselves became unnecessary.

III. Portraits of Exile: Copenhagen, June–July 1995

An epitaph written in water is no epitaph at all, as John Keats realized when he penned his own to read: "Here lies one whose name is writ in water." Unlike the nameless tombstone bearing these words and marking Keats's grave in Rome's Protestant cemetery, however, all traces of Denmark's extraordinary rescue of its Jews were erased by the very water that bore them to safe haven in Sweden. The water that made their rescue possible, and covered their tracks so well, also made a landscape of commemorative traces of this rescue impossible. As a memorial medium, in fact, water is more like fleeting time in its ephemerality than like a fixed landscape in its stasis, and so more emblematic of memory itself – always taking the shape of the vessel into which it is poured.

In the memorial and historical culture of Denmark, water is also much more. It was not only the road to rescue for Denmark's Jews during the Nazi occupation in October 1943, but it has always constituted Copenhagen's historical and economic *raison d'etre* as ancient seaport, quite literally the capital's historical life-source. It was with these thoughts in mind that Shimon Attie chose the Børsgraven canal in Copenhagen as his installation site for *Portraits of Exile* – a commemoration of the 50th anniversary of Denmark's liberation from the Nazis. This was not to be merely a self-congratulatory celebration of the war's end in the monolithic image of Denmark's heroic rescue of the Jews, however. For unlike the images of Jews projected back onto the buildings of the *Scheunenviertel* in Berlin, which seemed to animate otherwise inert surfaces, it was the somewhat stock and myth-hardened imagery of heroism itself that Attie animated – and thus dissolved – in the watery medium of Copenhagen's canals.

Here he installed a row of nine light boxes, each 1.8 by 1.6 meters, about 10 meters apart, and submerged nearly one meter below the water's surface some five meters from the bank of the canal. Eight of these light boxes were mounted with the transparency of a photograph depicting either the face of a Danish Jew rescued to Sweden or the face of a present day refugee now living in Denmark. One light box in the middle of the series was mounted with the transparent image of a sea-map charting the straits between Denmark and Sweden. Visible by night and day, these back-lighted faces stared up eerily, stirring with life as the water rippled over them. From a distance, the images seemed to float on the surface as orbs of light, a trail of stepping stones leading out to sea.

But the spectacle itself might have blinded viewers to details apparent only on closer inspection. When the wind and tides were perfectly still, and the water's surface took on a mirror-like sheen, just beyond the surface reflection of one's own face, other layers of these images came into view. Each image was of a different refugee, each overlaid with a different sign of exile: a portrait of a Danish Jewish man overlaid onto an image of a yellow Jewish star; another of a Danish Jewish woman overlaid onto a sea map; other faces of rescued Danish Jews overlaid onto images of a fishing boat used in the rescue and a commercial freighter. The middle image itself of the sea map was overlaid by two boats, one with Jews on their way to Sweden, another with present-day refugees coming to Denmark.

At which point, the narrative created in this sequence of images began to generate a decidedly double-edged memorial message, fraught with pride and shame. For the next image of a Bosnian Moslem refugee in turban is followed by a Bosnian woman overlaid by an image of the Flotel Europa moored one canal away – a notoriously over-crowded floating hotel ship crammed with refugees awaiting political asylum in Denmark, some of them waiting for years. The last two images consisted of the face of a Yugoslav man seemingly textured by an overlaid sea map and a Yugoslav woman whose face is blotched by the image of a passport entry stamp. Placed in the center of a topographical triad composed of the Foreign Ministry, the Danish Parliament, and the National Bank of Denmark, these portraits of exile seemed simultaneously to shine as commemorative and warning lights to the government.

This mixed memorial message was not intended to refute Denmark's reigning self-idealization as a perennial haven of refuge, but only to pierce the self-congratulatory side of this myth that blinds it to other, conflicting historical realities. Neither were such images juxtaposed to imply equivalence between refugees but to heighten a troubling contrast: where almost all Danish Jews were saved, not all Bosnians have found refuge, many more murdered at home than given safe-haven in Denmark or other European countries. At the same time, the artist showed how every national commemoration necessarily occludes as much history as it recalls. For even this greatest of mass-rescues during the Holocaust, once mythologized as part of the national character, has overshadowed another, less well-known historical fact of this era: that Denmark had refused to grant asylum to thousands of Jews attempting to flee Nazi Germany before the war.

Such a fact does not diminish the brilliance of Denmark's national heroism but only complicates it, thereby making it less myth-like, more real. Public memory here is as fraught and contradictory, as complex and multi-sided as the history being commemorated. In its mixed message, such an installation may even suggest that it is the memory of a mixed past that actually impels a nation toward new acts of rescue. For national memory of heroism, like the heroic act itself, stems from a mixture of motives – high, low and ambivalent.

IV. Brick by Brick: Cologne, November 1995

The physical sites of history are not the only potential sites of memory. In Attie's eyes, even the designs of household objects can recall the times of their origin and, by extension, the households from which they have been torn. Pieces of Bauhaus or Art Deco furniture come to stand as icons of an era that point beyond themselves to the dark age they passed through, to the owners – both killers and victims – they may have survived. Having re-animated public sites in Berlin and Dresden with images of their forgotten pasts, the artist would now turn his gaze into the more private, even intimate sanctum of the household, its objects transformed into their own accusing sites of memory.

In *Brick by Brick*, his installation just outside the doors of the Cologne Art Fair in November 1995, he projected images of simple household objects dating from turn of the century Germany onto the massive brick columns of the Rheinhalle. Projected so that they seemed almost to be materializing from within the brick columns, images of a Singer sewing machine, a late-19th century commode, a Bauhaus menorah, a Bauhaus dining room table, an overstuffed arm chair, and four other similarly aged objects confronted patrons of ART COLOGNE as they exited the exhibit hall. Though this particular crowd of collectors and connoisseurs would have recognized the general period of these objects' origins, neither they nor the artist could know the exact provenance of any given piece – gleaned by the artist from antique stores, as well as from Bauhaus and other catalogues. But this ambiguity was partly the point, for it was into this area of uncertainty that the artist projected his own preoccupations, assigning not a precise provenance but a generic, possible provenance to these and all pieces like them.

At the same time, this was a site-specific installation. For as Attie and his collaborator, Mathias Maile, made clear in a handbill passed out to visitors at the fair, the *Kölner Messegebäude* (Cologne Fair Building) had its own dark, if multi-layered and unacknowledged past. Built in 1923, the Cologne Fair Building had hosted its share of fairs, it was true, but after the Nazis came to power in 1933, it had also served as an examination center for German Army draftees, as well as a great hall for the ideological re-education of German school teachers. After launching the war in 1939, the Nazi government took control of the Fair Building and turned it first into a prisoner of war camp and then, in 1940, into a gathering and deportation site for Sinti and Roma. Still later, it served as a transfer station for Jews about to be deported to the east through the neighboring Deutz-Tief train station.

In fact, because the Nazis had taken over all such exhibition halls in Germany by this time, the fate of the Cologne Fair Building was no more ignoble than that of any other public hall in Germany. Rather, what had made this Fair Building special in Attie's eyes were the ways another part of its history seemed to find some continuity in the Art Fair itself. For some reason, the Cologne Art Fair, arguably the most prestigious of its kind in Germany today, opens every year on November 9th or 10th, the anniversary of *Kristallnacht* in 1938. Even more significant for Attie, however, was the building's use during the war as a storehouse for confiscated furniture and other household belongings of Jews who had either been forced to emigrate or deported to concentration camps. As the hall's stores filled up, Nazi Party officials would hold auctions open only to party members whose households had been damaged by Allied bombings. As chilling illustration, Attie photocopied an announcement for one such auction, Gothic script and all, as part of his handbill:

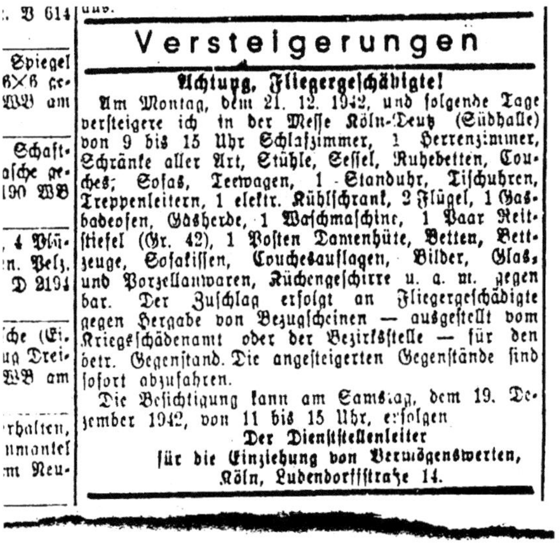

Versteigerungen

Achtung, Fliegergeschädigte!

Am Montag, dem 21. 12. 1942, und folgende Tage versteigere ich in der Messe Köln-Deutz (Südhalle) von 9 bis 15 Uhr Schlafzimmer, 1 Herrenzimmer, Schränke aller Art, Stühle, Sessel, Ruhebetten, Couches, Sofas, Teewagen, 1 Standuhr, Tischuhren, Treppenleitern, 1 elektr. Kühlschrank, 2 Flügel, 1 Gasbadeofen, Gasherde, 1 Waschmaschine, 1 Paar Reitstiefel (Gr. 42), 1 Posten Damenhüte, Betten, Bettzeuge, Sofakissen, Couchesauflagen, Bilder, Glas- und Porzellanwaren, Küchengeschirre u. a. m. gegen bar. Der Zuschlag erfolgt an Fliegergeschädigte gegen Hergabe von Bezugscheinen — ausgestellt vom Kriegsschädenamt oder der Bezirksstelle — für den betr. Gegenstand. Die angesteigerten Gegenstände sind sofort abzufahren.

Die Besichtigung kann am Samstag, dem 19. Dezember 1942, von 11 bis 15 Uhr, erfolgen

Der Dienststellenleiter
für die Einziehung von Vermögenswerten,
Köln, Ludendorffstraße 14.

A u c t i o n s

Attention, Bombing Victims!

On Monday, the 21st of December 1942 and following days, I will hold an auction at the Cologne-Deutz Fair (South Hall) from 9:00 A.M. to 3:00 P.M. Bedroom, men's bedroom, all kinds of wardrobes, tables, down beds, couches, sofas, teawagon, upright clock, table clock …

The list of objects included all the furnishings of any middle or upper-middle class German Jewish home. The rest of the handbill described how beginning in 1942, a slave labor camp was also installed on the fairgrounds in the form of a so-called "worker education camp." And finally, at the end of 1942, a satellite camp of Buchenwald composed of "SS Construction Crew III" was established on the Fair Grounds, supplying some 1,000 slave-laborers to the nearby Rheinish factories.

Thus greeted by this "counter-fair" on their way out of ART COLOGNE, patrons were forced to reconsider this site as something more than an exhibition hall for contemporary art. On display at the fair, but not for sale, Attie's installation redefined the hall as nexus of history, commerce, and memory. In a way, the Art Fair's organizers had foisted this link on Attie by scheduling its opening every year on the anniversary of *Kristallnacht*. Once inspired, however, Attie pursued the question that might logically follow "What happened to all the Jews of Germany?" That is, "What happened to all their household belongings and personal effects?" Further implied questions include not only "Where were you during the war?" But also, "To whom did that table belong before the war? Is it an ill-gotten gain, a Nazi-sanctioned piece of war-booty? Or was it passed down innocently from one generation to the next?" Instead of suggesting answers, the artist let such questions float in the space of the art fair, between his installation and bustling art patrons. Contemporary German collectors were now confronted uneasily with the possibility that these objects had even been distributed among their own households.

What makes such an installation so subversive is the way it plants the seeds of doubt in every such piece: the more authentic it is, the more it might remind its current owner of its possible provenance. Even perfectly "innocent" pieces might now echo with the voices of the dead, and by their very design, such pieces begin to accuse their owners. In effect, the provenance of antiques from this era makes them not only valuable but historical. In *Brick by Brick*, the artist has thus stigmatized an entire generation of household objects, and in so doing, he transformed each piece from mere memento into an accusing memento mori.

V. The Neighbor Next Door: Amsterdam, December 1995

Like the people of other nations, the Dutch tend to remember their World War II past as it congeals around a few well-chosen images: in their case, of course, Anne Frank constitutes the central memorial icon. But as a remarkably self-critical generation of new historians in Holland has already made clear, the Dutch self-idealization in the image of Anne Frank has always been double-edged: she reminds the Dutch both that they helped hide her family from the Nazis and that they also betrayed her. As these historians are quick to point out, despite the national mythology of the "sheltering Dutch," a higher percentage of its Jews – over 80% – was murdered during the Holocaust than any other nation's except for Poland's.

In keeping with Holland's own capacity for self-critique, Attie's Amsterdam installation, *The Neighbor Next Door*, attempted to remind the Dutch of the essential gulf between the historical record and national memory of the Holocaust, the essential double-sidedness of "the neighbor next door." At the same time, he hoped to suggest that for the estimated 100,000 illegal immigrants hiding in Holland today, the myth of "the neighbor next door" lives on in decidedly mixed fashion, as they find economic refuge in a land that needs but does not necessarily want them. It now reflects their contemporary reality, as well, as they peek from behind closed curtains, or look over their shoulders on the way to or from illegal jobs.

For one week in the middle of December 1995, Attie mounted 16mm film projectors inside the windows of three different flats along Prinsengracht, the canal-street in central Amsterdam on which Anne Frank's family and an estimated 155 other groups hid during World War II. From 5:00 p.m. in the early evening to 1:00 a.m. in the morning, Attie beamed onto the street below short film loops from footage shot clandestinely from nearby windows by those in hiding during the Nazi occupation. Even in darkness, the grainy film footage appeared shadowy and fleeting. In one 10-second loop projected from Prinsengracht 572, the stiff, grey figures of a Nazi funeral cortege filed into view on its way to bury a Dutch-Nazi collaborator assassinated by the resistance; at Prinsengracht 468, wet cobblestones flickered silently with the images of a military band decked out in the insignia of the Dutch Nazi Party, marching in an endless 6-second loop. Only the images of passing German soldiers giving the Heil Hitler salute flitting across the sidewalk in front of Prinsengracht 514 had been from film shot by Nazi propagandists, now mocked by the robotic repetition of the loop itself.

In these projections, Attie hoped to convey how the world looked *from* the hiding place, as opposed to how the hiding place looked to the outside world through free Dutch eyes. In addition, he tried to try to show how hiding was experienced by those who hid: already a kind of internment, for some the first of many incarcerations on the way to concentration and death. Here the national image of sheltering was being turned inside-out, the lens turned back on those for whom the "neighbor next door" had become more a self-aggrandizing image than a reality. The image of the sheltered was now displaced by moving images of what the sheltered saw: Dutch bystanders, collaborators, and Nazis. By re-animating the past of those supposedly rescued, Attie could reiterate the national myth even as he unlocked its hold on the past.

VI. The Walk of Fame: Krakow, June–July 1996

In his Krakow project, *The Walk of Fame*, Attie suggests that art itself can check the excesses of art, that instead of blurring the line further between history and its later representations, art can re-draw this line and that, through parody, it can discourage a society from unwittingly displacing history as it happened with history as it appears in the movies. He was inspired, he says, not by the ways Steven Spielberg's film, *Schindler's List* might have passed itself off as history, but rather by the potential confusion in tourists' minds wrought by an officially sanctioned tour in Krakow called "Retracing 'Schindler's List'."

In this tour, organized by Franciszek Palowski, a Polish journalist who had interviewed Spielberg for Polish television and later wrote a book on the filming of *Schindler's List*, tourists are invited to visit the sites of film-making in and around Krakow in order to learn more of the actual history of Schindler's list and its telling in cinema. As a guide, Palowski is very careful to distinguish between the sites of actual history and the sites where Spielberg chose to film this history. Nevertheless, Attie fears that the mere possibility of such a tour throws "authentic historical sites, events and individuals into open competition with their celluloid copies in determining our understanding of history." It is one thing to add the history of the film to the history of events, another to displace the history of events with the history of the film.

Moreover, Attie worries that "As actual history becomes conflated with cinematic fiction, it becomes more and more difficult to distingish between the two." In fact, underlying Attie's misgivings here seems to be not just the confusion in mind wrought by such a tour but the ways that such a tour is, in many ways, more appealing to tourists in the thrall of celebrity history than history itself. For when all is said and done, tourists may indeed prefer visiting the sites of *their* cinematic experience of the Holocaust to seeing the sites of *others'* actual Holocaust experiences. After all, their only "real" experience of the Holocaust is the "reel" experience of the movie itself. Having survived the film, in effect, they return as vicarious pilgrims to the cinematic sites, just as survivors of the camps return to the sites of their actual suffering. If the movie becomes our history of the Holocaust, then the movie sets become the places where "history is made." And once we are invited to visit the sites of filming as if they were the places where "history is made," it is too short a step toward confusing the history made in this film for history itself.

Because he is a filmmaker and not a documentarian, Spielberg need not have hewn to original sites of history for his fictional account any more than the novelist need rely on notarized testimony for dialogue. The aim was never to film authentic sites but to make the sites he filmed look authentic: this is what film-makers do, and Spielberg did it brilliantly. In addition to building his own concentration camp set nearby the real one, Spielberg found a plethora of authentic-looking old squares and buildings in which to shoot his Krakow ghetto scenes. As its residents know well and its tourists happily discover, Krakow's great charm as a tourist center stems from the fact that it has never been bombed or otherwise damaged in the numberless wars and occupations. Only new buildings made the authentic center of the Jewish ghetto at Zgoda Square unfit for shooting sequences that had actually taken place there. These scenes were shot instead on Szeroka street, the center of the former Jewish district in Kazimierz.

We also learn from "Retracing 'Schindler's List'" that because the ghetto scenes at Zgoda Square in the Podgorze district were filmed in Kazimierz across the river, Spielberg had to reverse the actual direction of the march of Ghetto Jews, so that they flowed over the bridge *into* his filmic ghetto in Kazimierz and not out of Kazimierz over the Vistula into Podgorze, as they had originally. Also of cultural interest here is the plot of land Spielberg chose for his gargantuan movie set of the Plaszow concentration camp: the site of the former Jewish cemetery on Jerozolimska (Jerusalem) Street in Podgorze.

As late as April 1995, Attie's plan for an installation in Krakow looked entirely different. In a project then entitled *Routes of Silence*, the artist had hoped to mount slide projectors on the trams in Krakow that still run through what had been the Jewish ghetto there during the war, beaming images of the old ghetto back onto the present sites. In addition, he had planned to affix light boxes along the route to show "images from the ghetto, as well as images relating to Poland's post-communist struggle to be assimilated into the West and the challenges the country faces today with both old and new forms of racism."[3] But on his arrival in Krakow, he found the situation on the ground to be much more interesting, and more complicated, than his critique of Poland's wartime memory might have allowed. Though his original plan had been supported by both the city of Krakow and the local Goethe Institute, once the artist got wind of *Retracing Schindler's List*, his project metamorphosed from a critique of Poland's wartime memory into a critique of the dangers implicit in over-mediation itself. Unable to bear the confusion of movie and historical sites, Attie abandoned his own preconceived project and embarked on an alternative installation, one he hoped would expose the fascination for the filmic at the expense of the historical. As a result, *The Walk of Fame* may be as much an overall critique of Holocaust-by-mediation as it is of a specific displacement of historical by cinematic reality.

To this end, he installed 24 simulated five-point terrazzo stars, copies of the famous stars lining Hollywood Boulevard's "Walk of Fame," on Szeroka Street where Spielberg had constructed his ghetto movie-set: what Attie calls "ground-zero" for the conflation of movie history and historical fact. Instead of recalling the movie stars enshrined so famously on Hollywood Boulevard, however, Attie substituted the names of Jews who had actually been on Schindler's list, abbreviating the first names in order not to offend the memory of actual victims. By remembering actual victims as if they were worth remembering because they had now become Hollywood stars, Attie parodically repeated this flow of history into celebrity, mocking it, and thereby hoping to expose its insidiousness.

At the same time, Attie takes pains to explain that he has not directed this project against the individuals who survived Schindler's list and the celebrity it has brought some of them; nor would he make Spielberg's film a target of his countermemorial installation. Rather, in his words, "its intention was to highlight and critically reflect the larger problematic eclipsing of historical fact by cinematic fiction," by which the unfurling movie's reel is mistaken for the real. On display in Krakow during the months of June and July 1995, these purple stars were embedded into the square in front of the Old Synagogue and Jewish Museum, each with a small motion picture camera and a name like H. Blumentricht or J.H. Borenstein. Riven by cracks that seemed continuous with the surrounding stones, they appeared old, worn and permanently part of the square. Instead of the memorial icon of a yellow star, these survivors were commemorated with the purple, terrazzo stars of Hollywood celebrities, an echo of that moment at the end of *Schindler's List*, when the actual survivors appeared with the stars who "played" them.

As an artist, Shimon Attie is all too aware of his own dependence on the art of others for his knowledge of the Holocaust. As a Jewish-American born after the war, he knows the Holocaust only by indirection, by the efforts of survivors, historians, and artists to pass down their knowledge to him. But while he acknowledges this necessarily vicarious relationship to Holocaust history on the one hand, he is still nettled by the possible consequences of what might be called the over-mediation of events. He fears, rightly, that a generation after the Holocaust could still come to mistake *their* hyper-mediated experiences of the Holocaust for the Holocaust itself, that events will come to be displaced altogether by their representations.

This is, he acknowledges, a conundrum. For since these representations of the Holocaust *are* all that those removed from events will ever know of the genocide, what is to keep art from usurping the authority of historical actuality? Moreover, if artists and filmmakers insist on keeping the boundaries between their art and actual events as fuzzy as possible, all toward the aesthetic (but not necessarily historical) end of making their art seem as convincing and entertaining as possible, then what is to save the next generation from losing the ability to discriminate between what they know, how they know it, and what actually happened? Instead of a simple answer to this, the next generation's defining preoccupation, Shimon Attie has offered a series of installations that work through the dilemma itself, that examine our role in the space between a site and its past, between history and memory.

Notes

1 Pierre Nora, "Between Memory. and History: *Les Lieux de Memoire,*" *Representations* 26, Spring 1989: 19.

2 Shimon Attie, *The Writing on the Wall Project,* in *The Writing on the Wall: Proiections in Berlin's Jewish Quarter* (Heidelberg: Edition Braus, 1994), page 9.

3 From "An Artist Projects a Ghostly Past," by Ferdinand Protzman, *The Forward,* 21 April 1995: 10.

PORTRAITS OF EXILE
June–July, 1995

Submerged light boxes. Nine 1.6 x 1.8 meter light boxes mounted with "dura-trans" (transparency) photographs submerged 1 meter under water, Børsgraven Canal, Copenhagen, Denmark.

Realized in collaboration with Mathias Maile based on a concept by Shimon Attie organized and produced by BizArt, Copenhagen

Denmark, and Copenhagen, have a unique history, being the only country occupied by the Nazis to save almost it's entire Jewish community. The rescue of October 1943, when thousands of Jews were saved by being secretly shepherded on fishing boats to Sweden, is an important part of Danish identity and is a contrast to today's hesitant and ambivalent refugee politics.
Today, Copenhagen plays a central role as a gathering point and way station for refugees from the Balkans and the former Soviet Union. Denmark's liberal social welfare state has made Copenhagen an attractive destination for many of these refugees. The reality, however, is different – with political refugees waiting for years, being stowed away in a crowded "hotel" ship or in refugee hostels, while asylum applications are being processed and delayed.
Given this coming together of issues related to water, history, and rescue, both past and present, nine large (1.6 x 1.8 meter) light boxes mounted with "dura-trans" (transparency) photographs were submerged approximately 1 meter under water in the Børsgraven canal near the Danish parliament building. The images, being back-lit, were visible 24 hours a day. *Portraits of Exile* was underwater for approximately 7 weeks.

21 Installation Shot. On light box in foreground: *Present day refugee from the former Yugoslavia with Danish entry stamp on passport*

23 Present day refugee from the former Yugoslavia with Danish entry stamp on passport

24 Danish Jew rescued to Sweden in Oct. 1943 with commercial freight ship

25 Present day refugee with dormitory ship ("Flotel Europa") used to house refugees in Copenhagen harbor

26 Danish Jew rescued to Sweden in Oct. 1943 with boat used in the rescue

27 Danish Jew rescued to Sweden in Oct. 1943 with boat used in the rescue

28 Present day refugee from the former Yugoslavia with sea map of channel between Denmark and Sweden (looking towards Denmark)

29 Danish Jew rescued to Sweden in Oct. 1943 with sea map of channel between Denmark and Sweden (looking towards Sweden)

30 Danish Jew rescued to Sweden in Oct. 1943 with commercial freight ship

31 Present day refugee with dormitory ship ("Flotel Europa") used to house refugees in Copenhagen harbor

32 Danish Jew rescued to Sweden in Oct. 1943 with Nazi "Jew" star

33 Danish Jew rescued to Sweden in Oct. 1943 with commercial freight ship

34 Present day refugee from the former Yugoslavia with Danish entry stamp on passport

35 Present day refugee with dormitory ship ("Flotel Europa") used to house refugees in Copenhagen harbor

36 In foreground: *Danish Jew rescued to Sweden in Oct. 1943 with sea map of channel between Denmark and Sweden (looking towards Sweden)*

37 In foreground: *Danish Jew rescued to Sweden in Oct. 1943 with boat used in the rescue*

38 In foreground: *Danish Jew rescued to Sweden in Oct. 1943 with Nazi "Jew" star*

39 In foreground: *Present day refugee from the former Yugoslavia with Danish entry stamp on passport*

41 Installation Shot

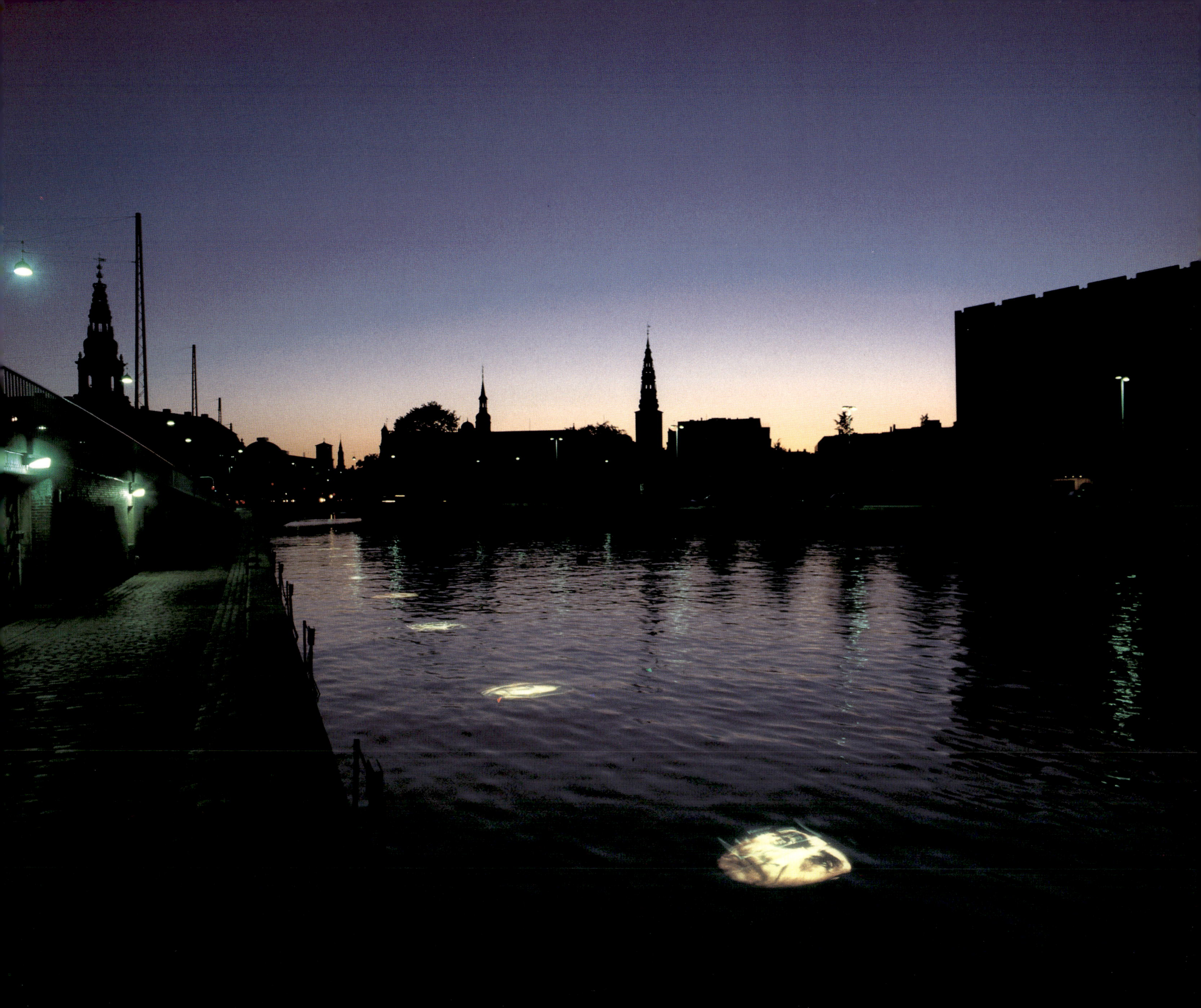

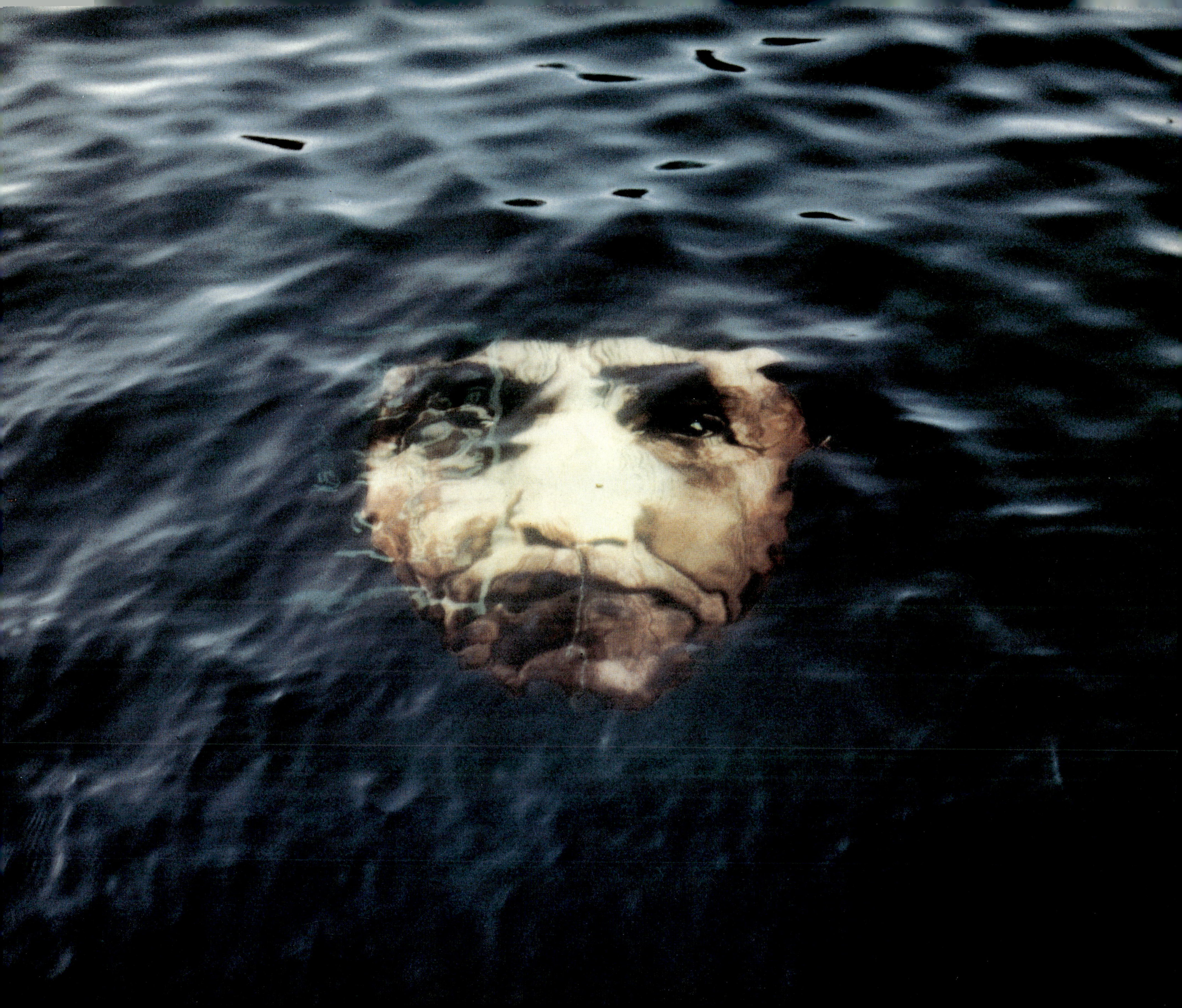

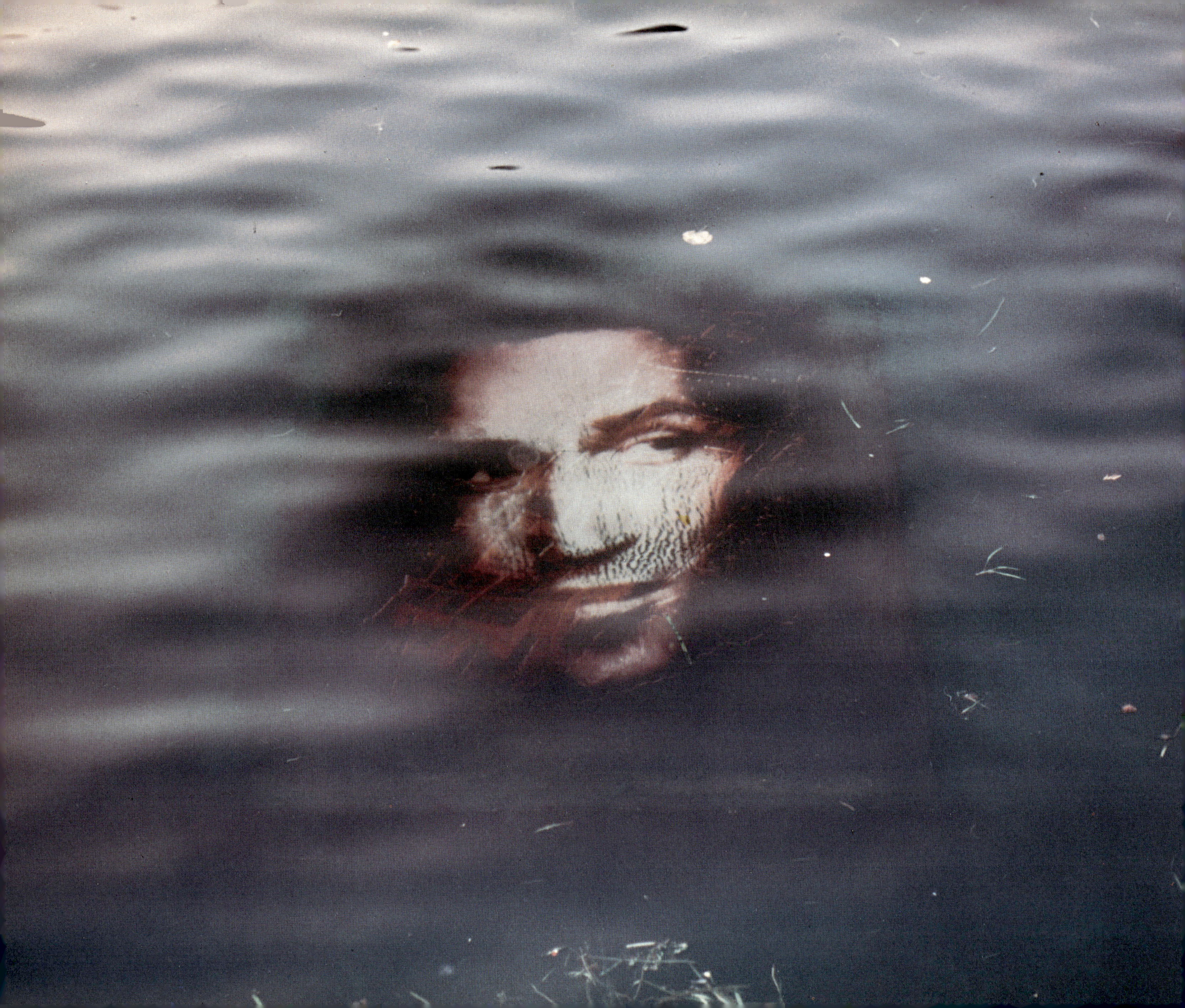

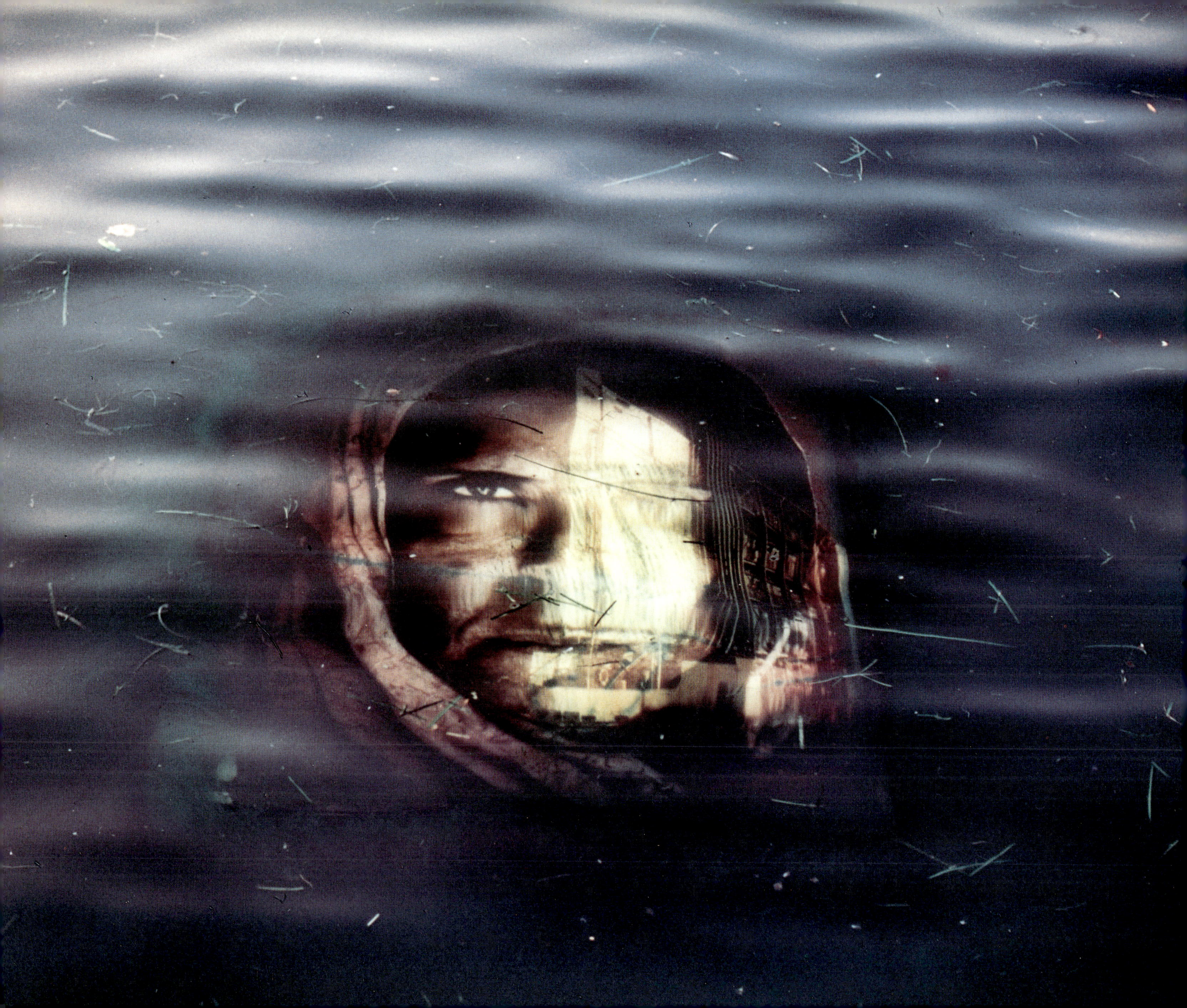

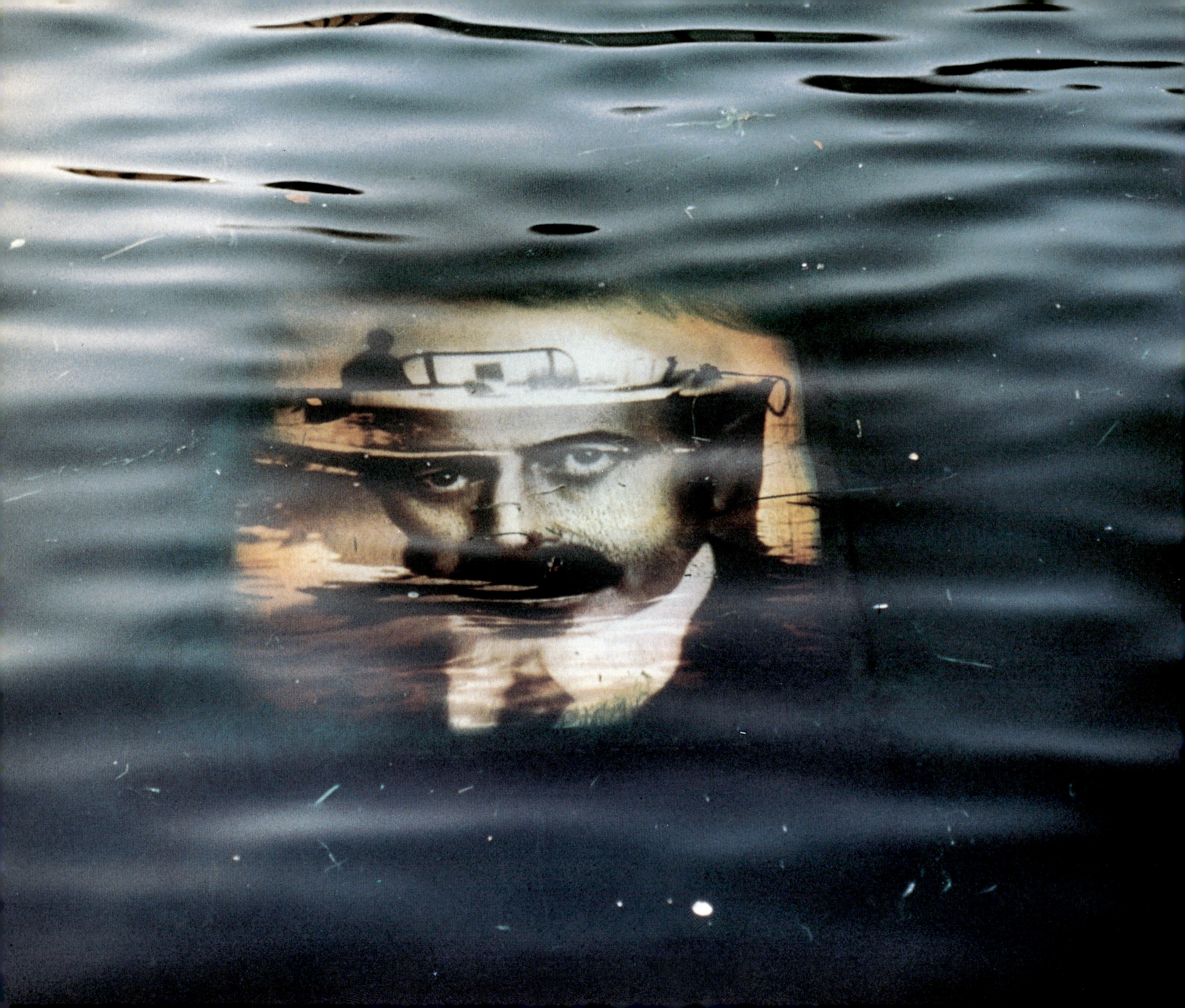

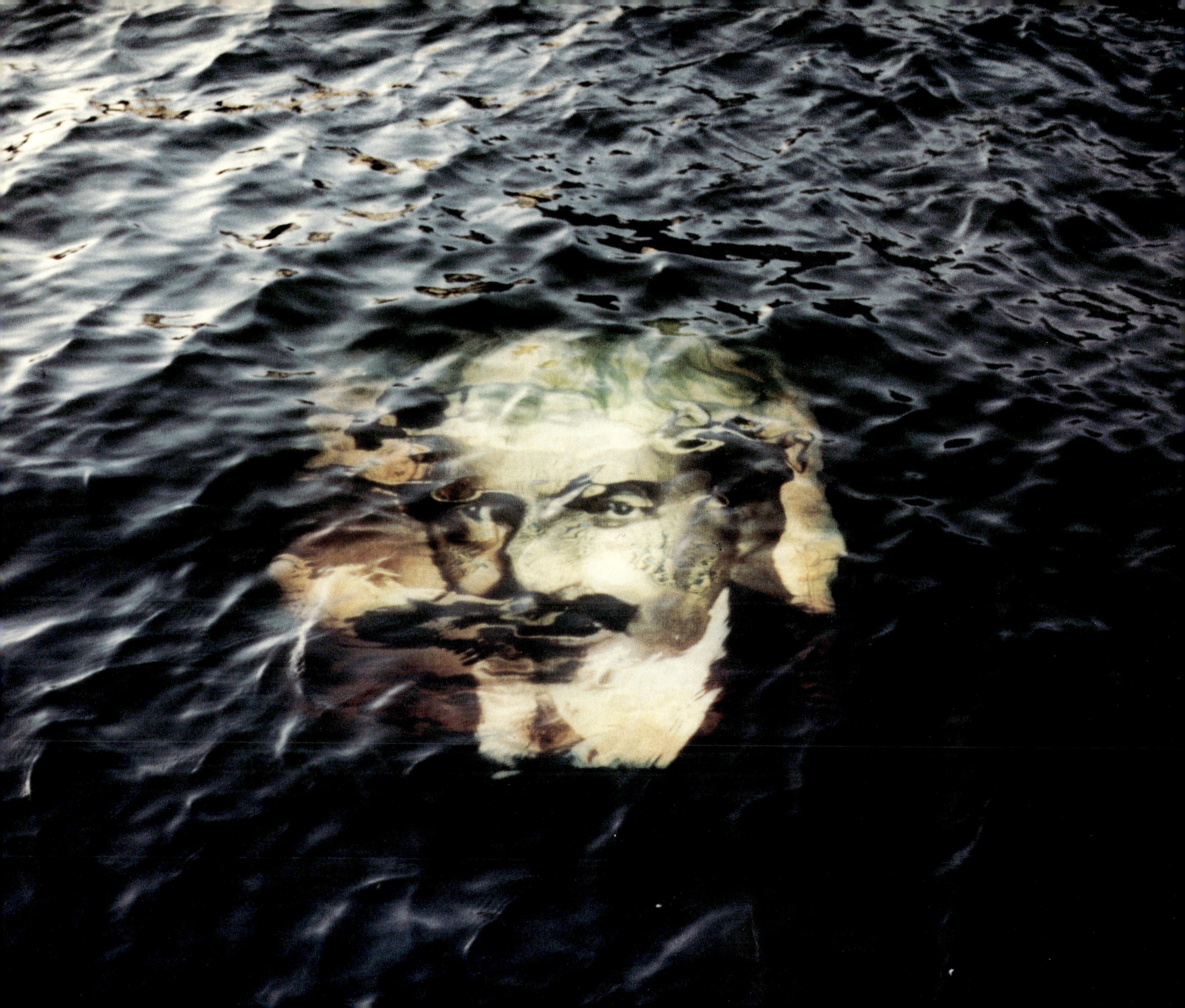

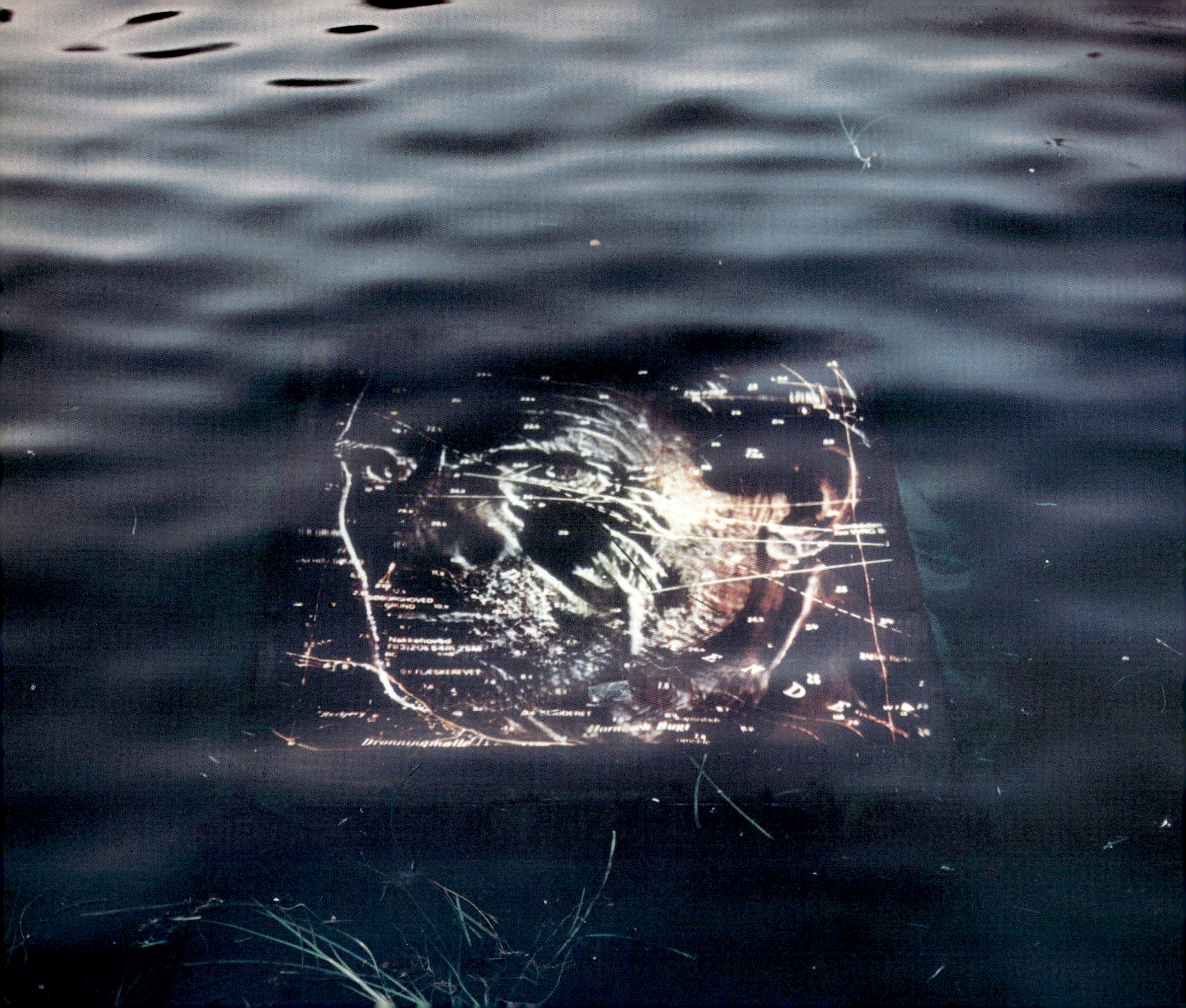
Nakkehoved
FLASKEREVET
Hornbæk Bugt

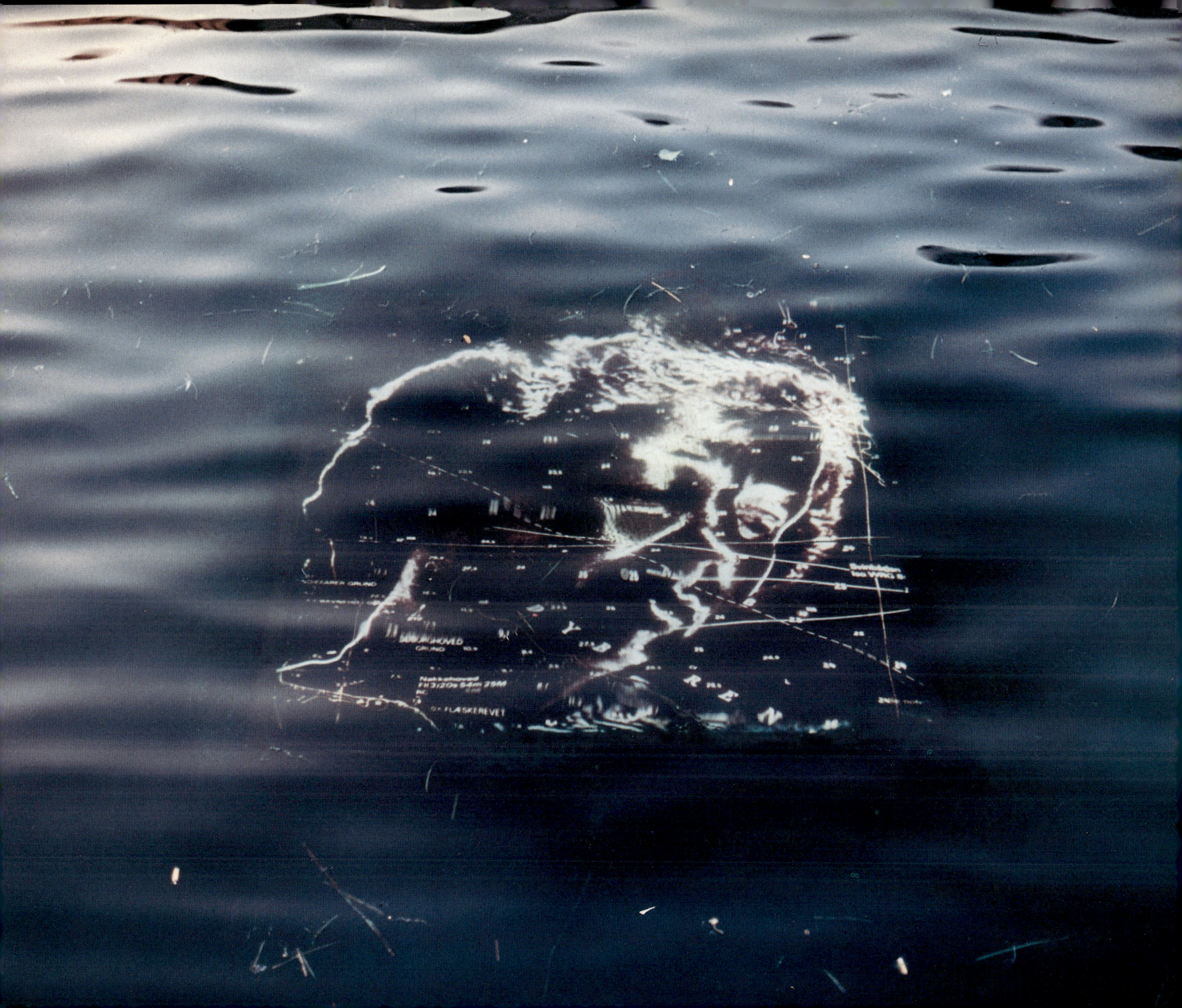
FLÆSKEREVET

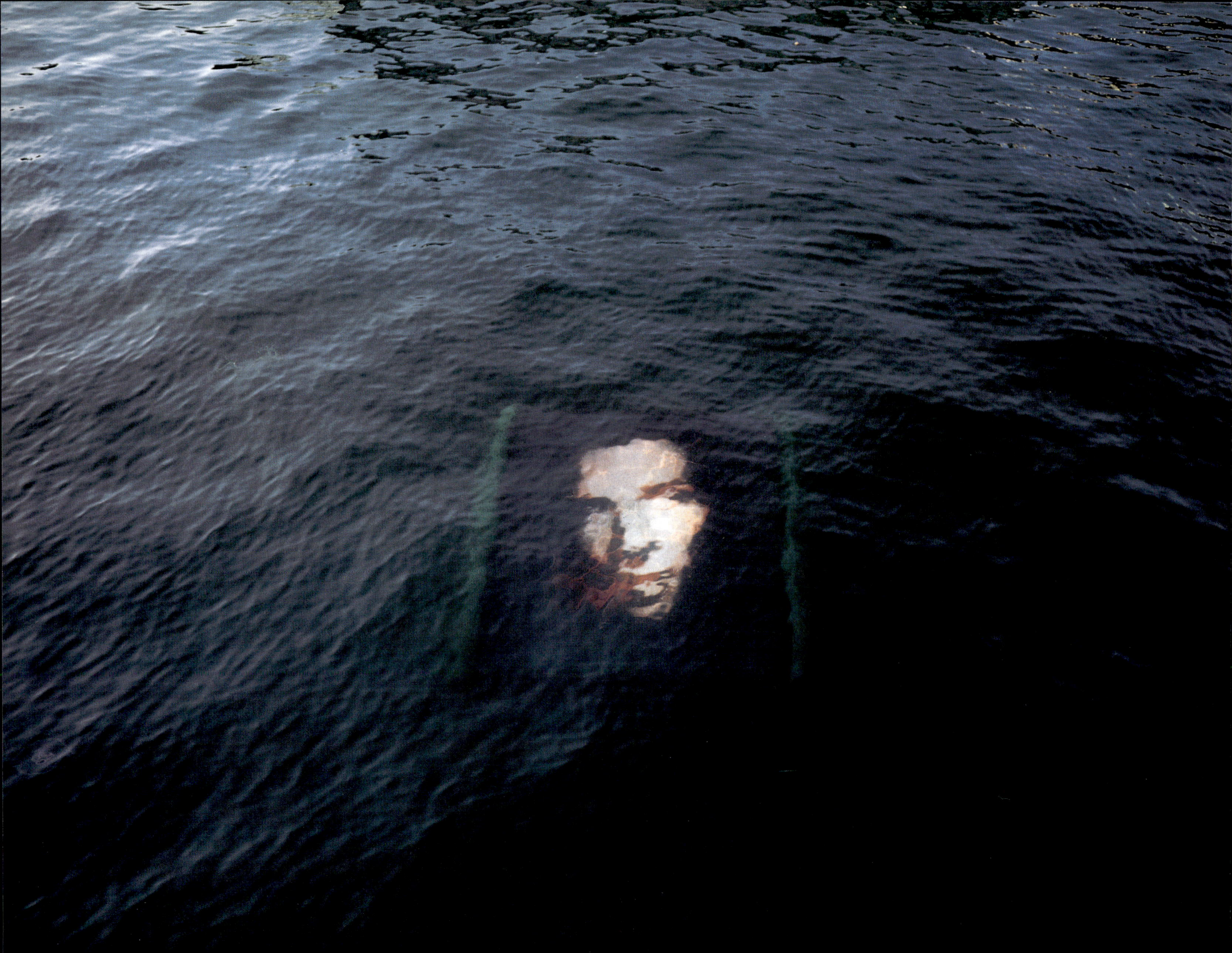

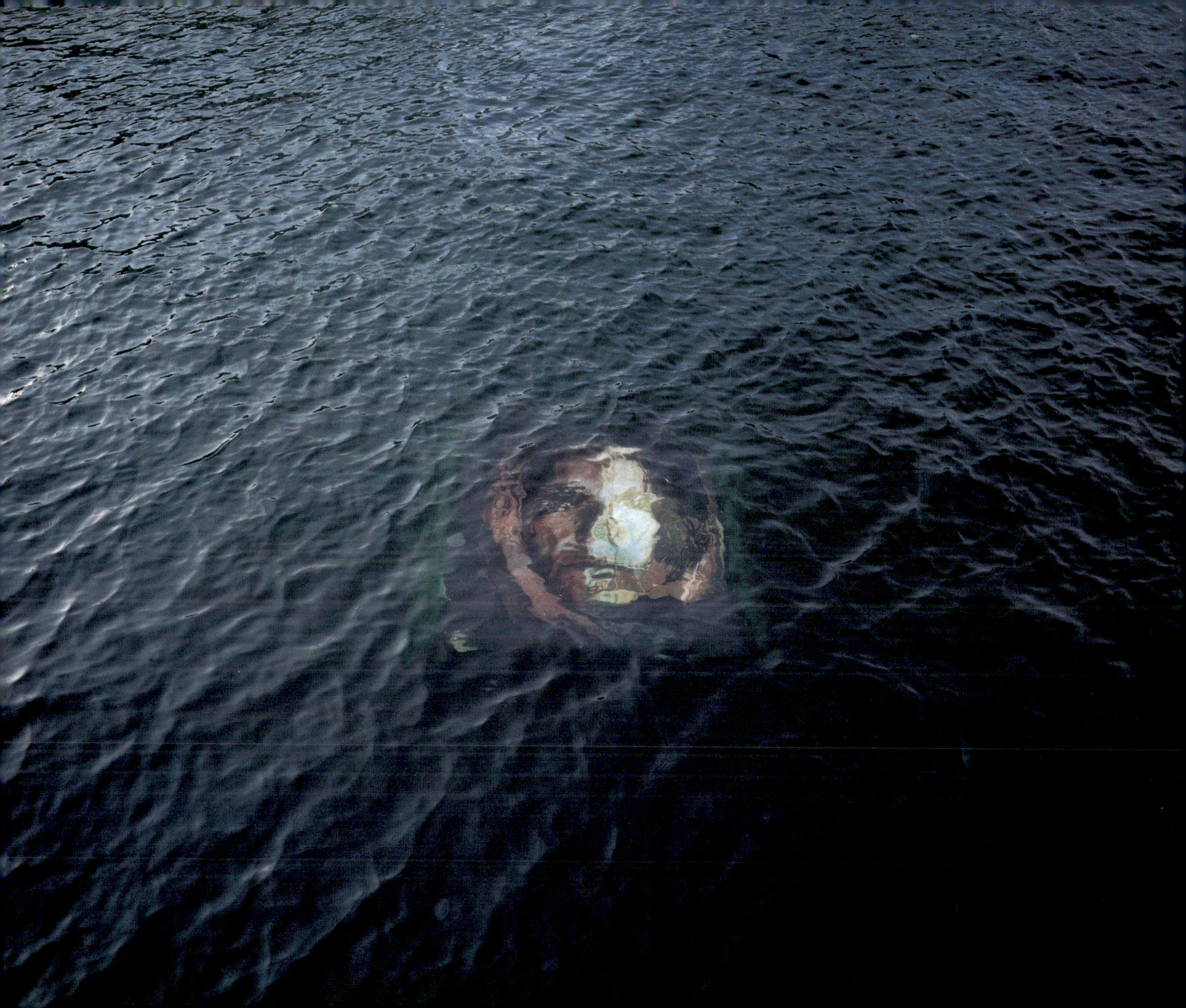

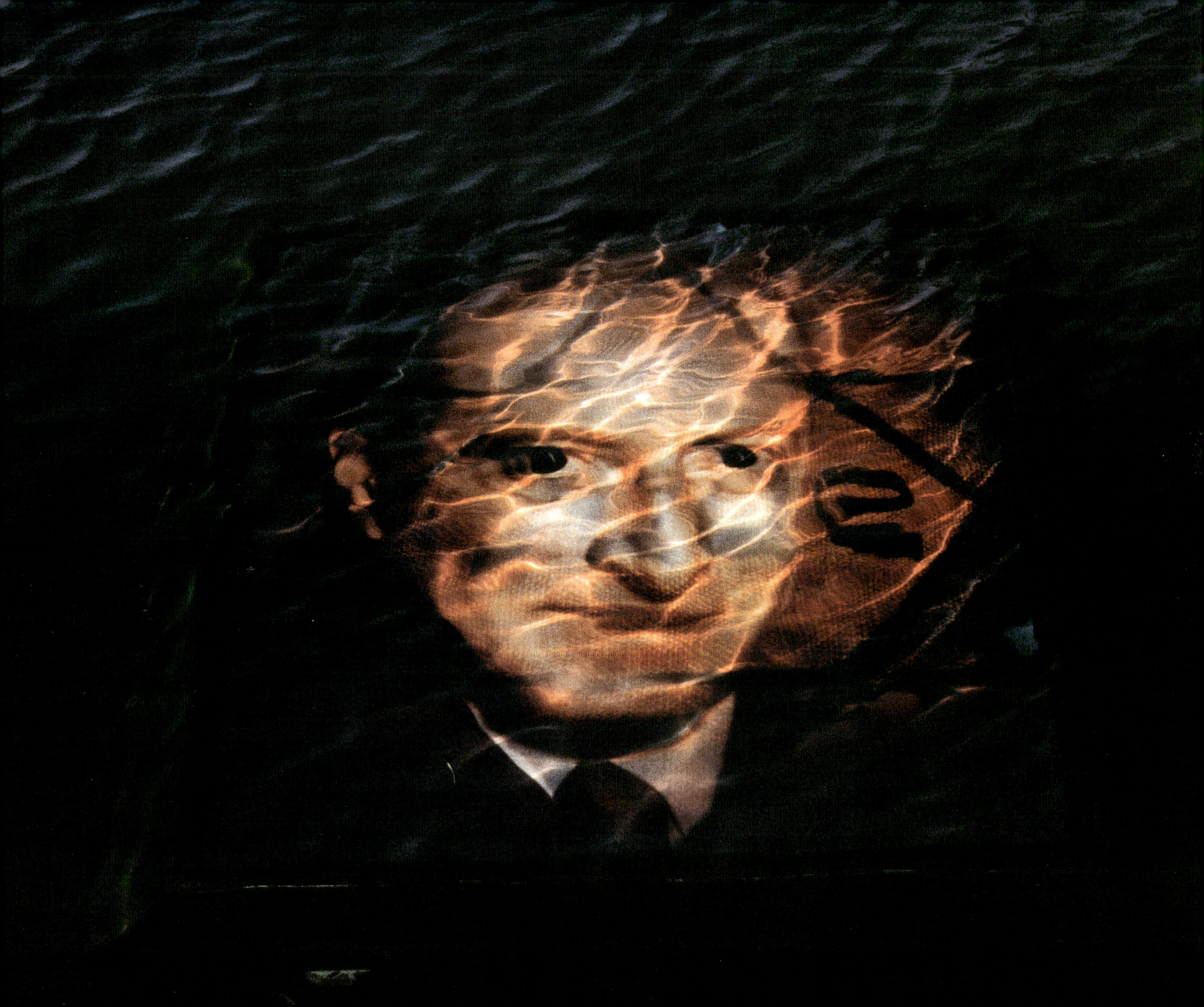

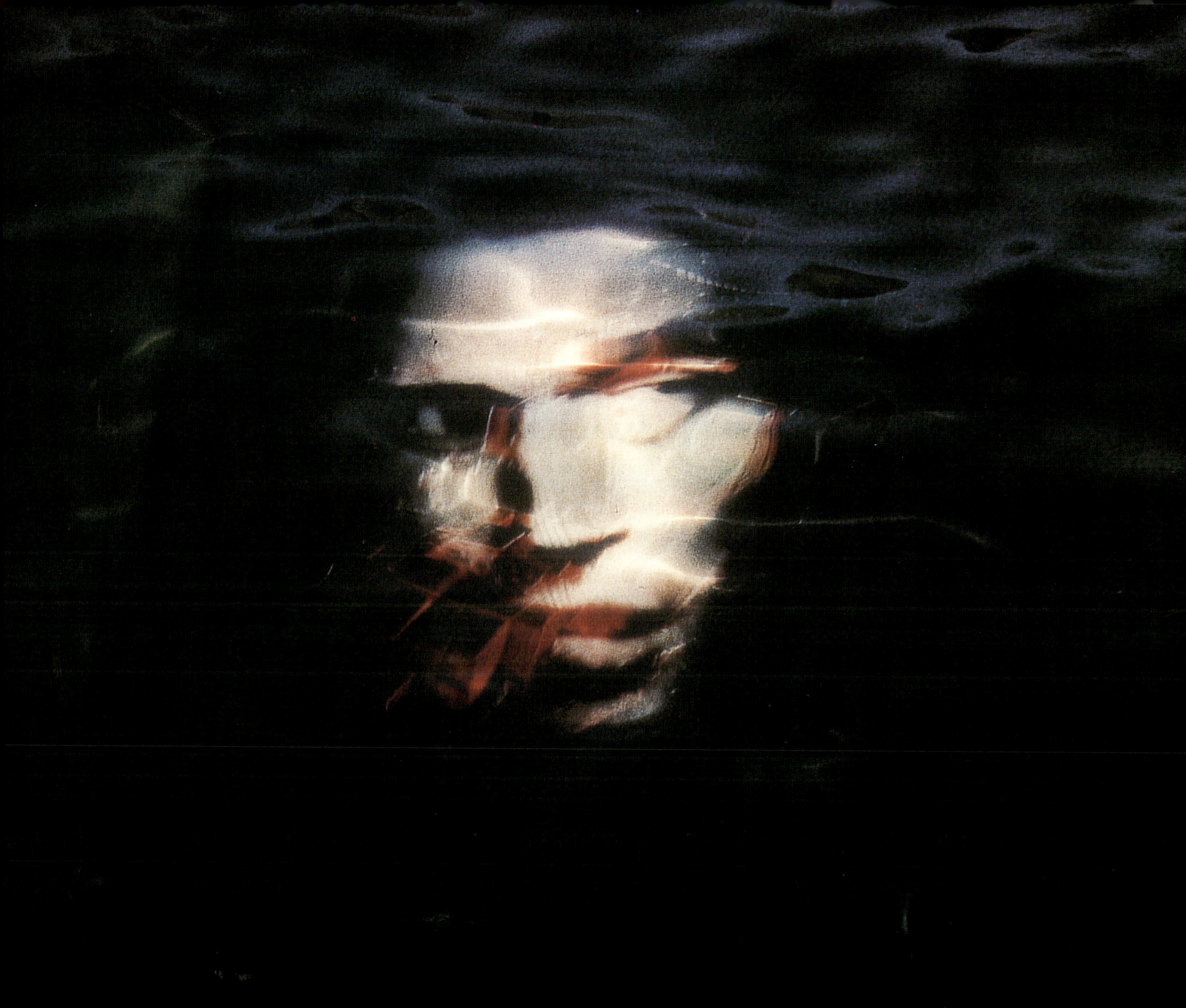

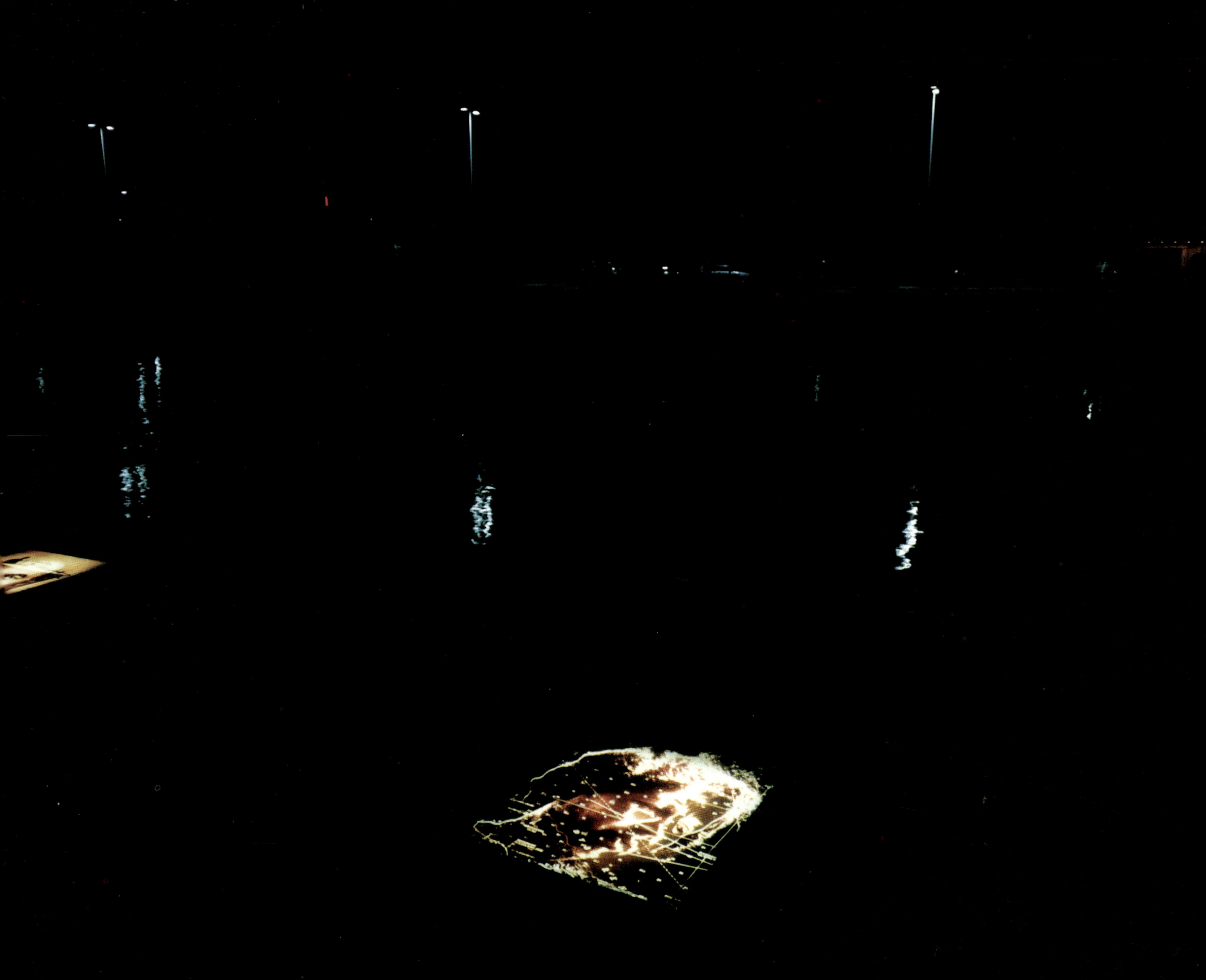

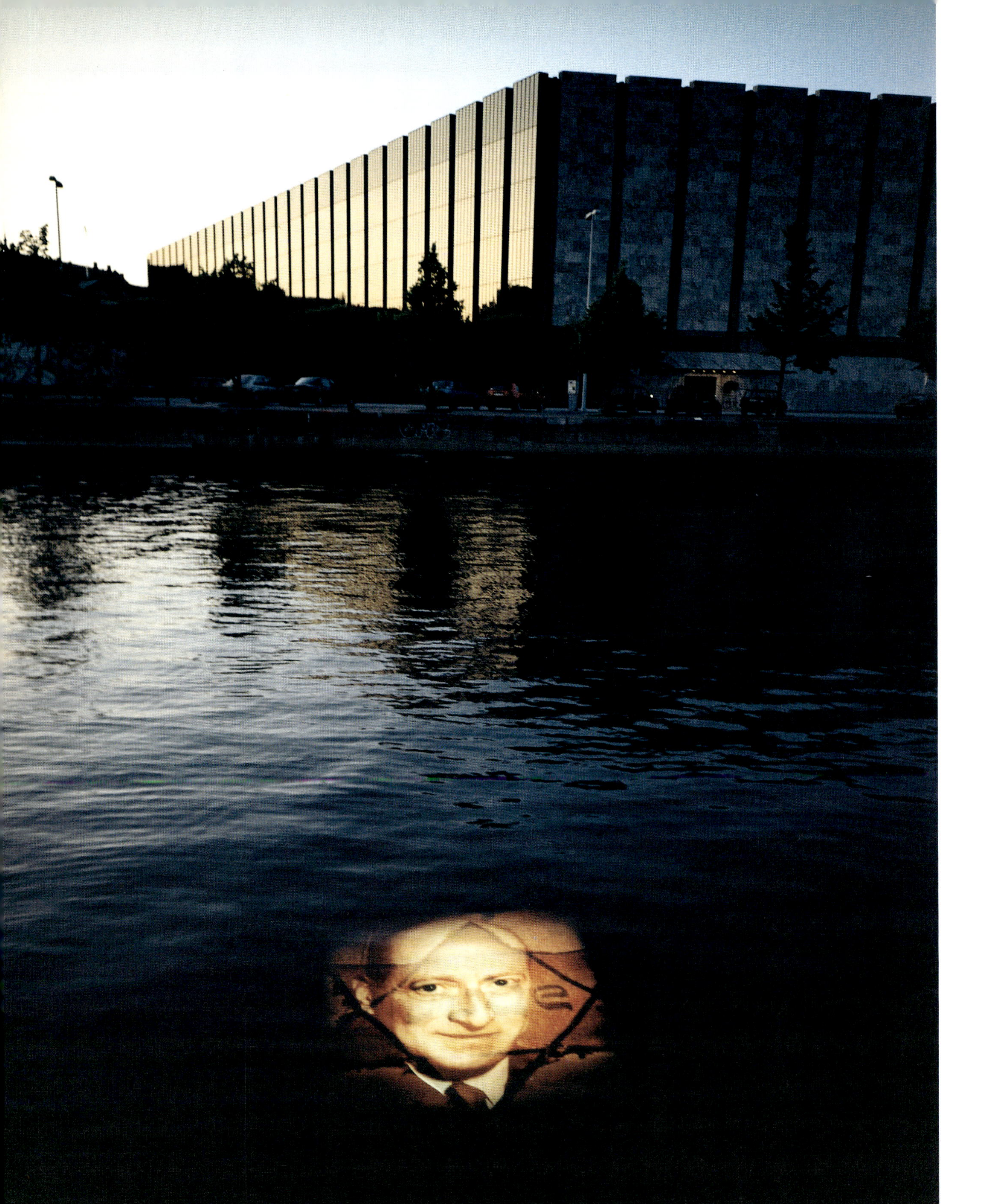

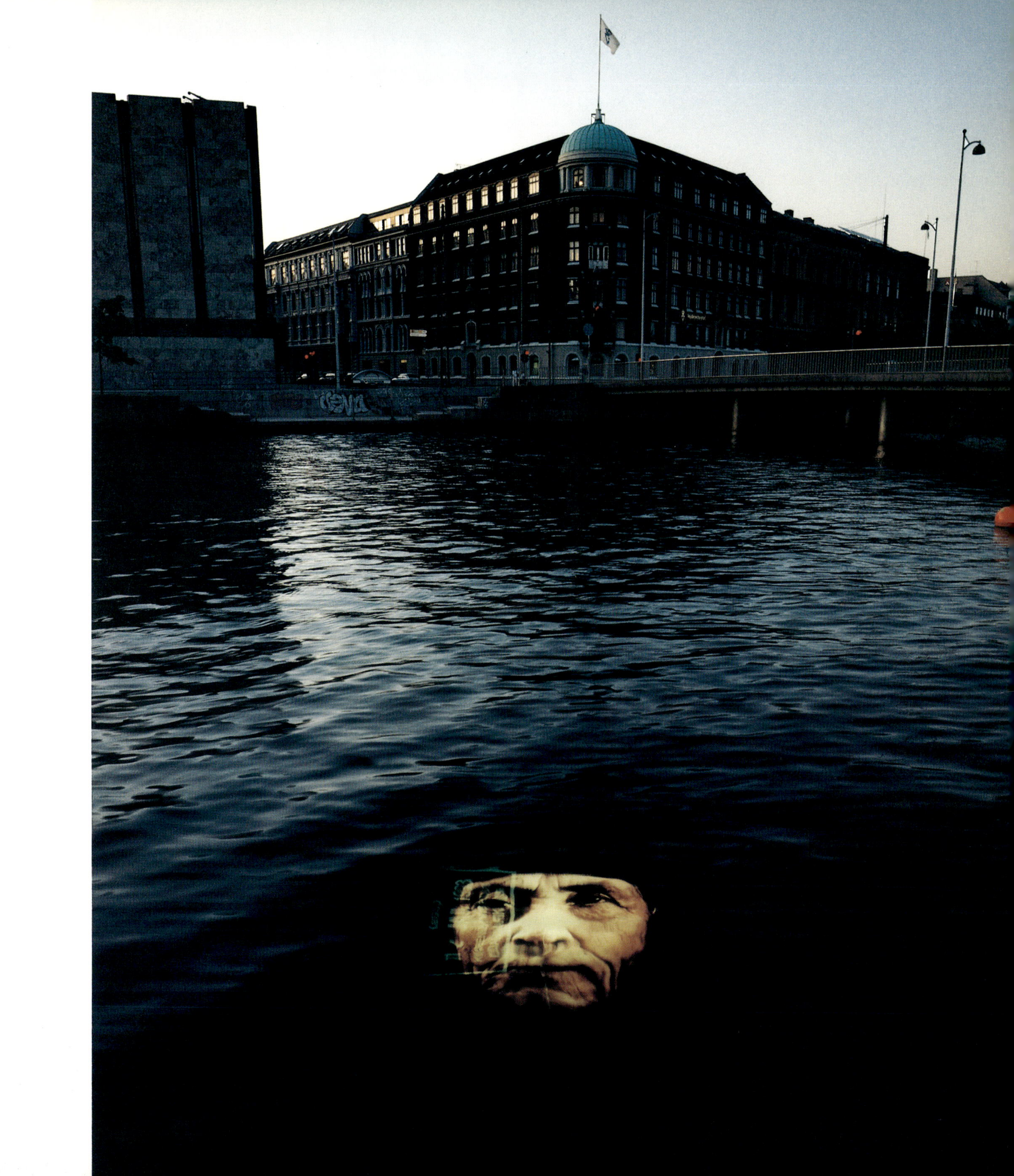

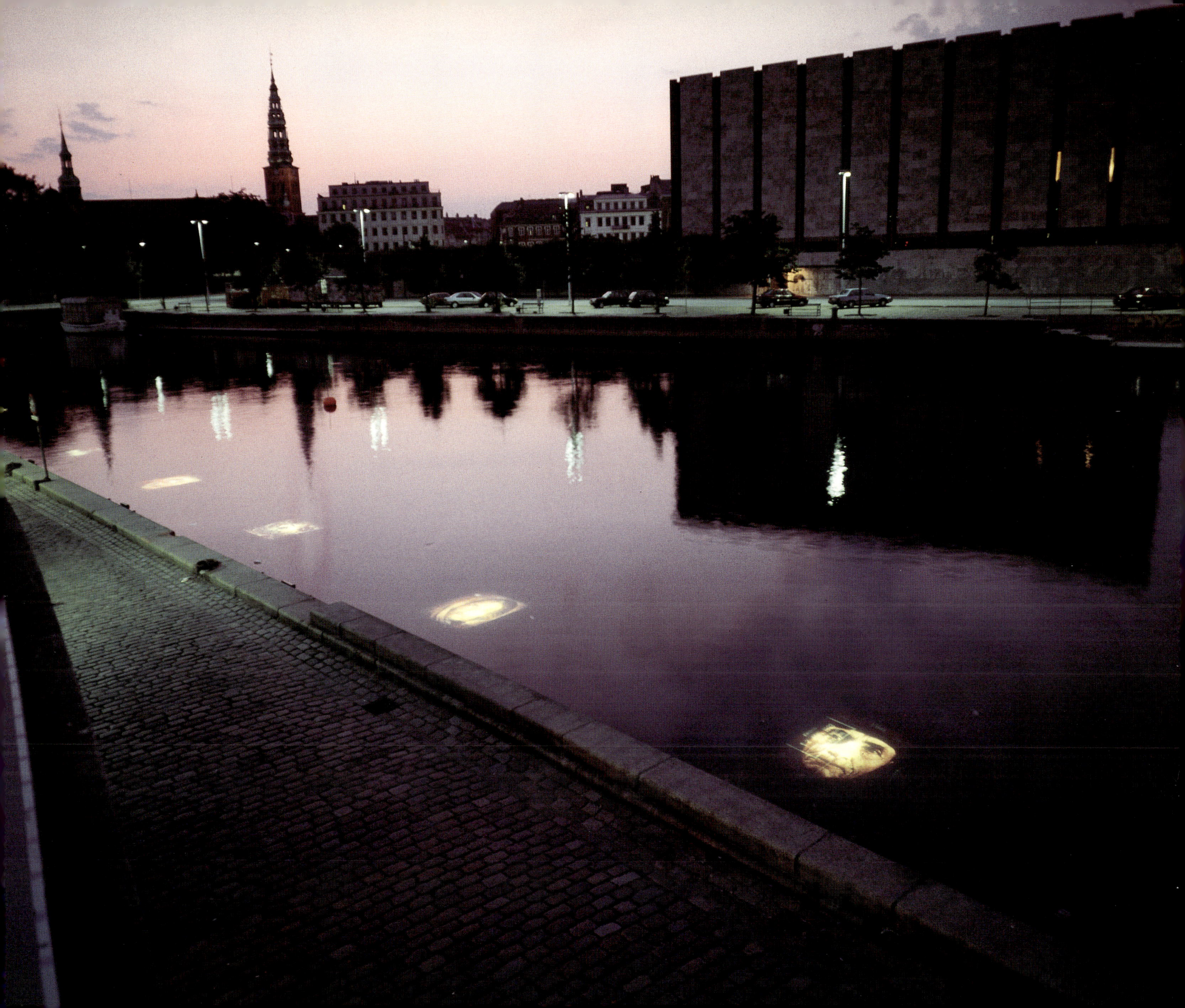

THE NEIGHBOR NEXT DOOR
December, 1995

Film projections from former hiding places, ca. 1943 (filmed from hidden cameras), Amsterdam, the Netherlands.

Organized and produced by the Paradox Foundation, Rotterdam

During the years of Nazi occupation, more than 80% of Amsterdam's Jewish citizens were deported to death camps and never returned. Due to a few well publicized instances in which Jews were hidden by their fellow Dutch citizens – the most widely known among these being the case of Anne Frank – a mythology of the "sheltering" Dutch has developed. Often overlooked is the fact that many Dutch collaborated with the Nazis and turned in their Jewish neighbors to the Gestapo.

Today in Amsterdam, thousands of illegal immigrants, without proper residence papers, are also in hiding, fearing deportation should they be discovered. The Netherlands, like much of the rest of Western Europe, is struggling with the issue of how wide it should open its doors to needy immigrants, given the already perceived strain on the country's social system.

The Neighbor Next Door took place at a number of addresses on the Prinsengracht where Jews and others were hidden during the war. For *The Neighbor Next Door*, 16 millimeter film projectors were placed inside a window at each former hiding place. Portions of original archival film footage were projected onto the street below. The footage used for the project had been secretly shot from above during the years of Nazi occupation by individuals in hiding with hidden cameras.* Thus, images of the outside world as they appeared from the vantage point of those formerly in hiding were simulated and projected out into a public space.

Much of the footage shot from hidden cameras tends to shed an unflattering light on Dutch behavior during the war, as many of the film clips recorded Dutch collaboration with their German occupiers.

The Neighbor Next Door was realized with the technical assistance of Karlheinz Reimann. *The Neighbor Next Door* took place December 15–22, 1995.

* the sole exception was the footage used at Prinsengracht 514, which had been shot as part of a german propaganda film.

45 Prinsengracht 514: *German soldiers in formation*

47 Prinsengracht 572: *Passing funeral*

49 Prinsengracht 572: *Passing funeral*

51 Prinsengracht 468: *Passing military band*

53 Prinsengracht 468: *Passing military band*

55 Prinsengracht 468: *Passing military band*

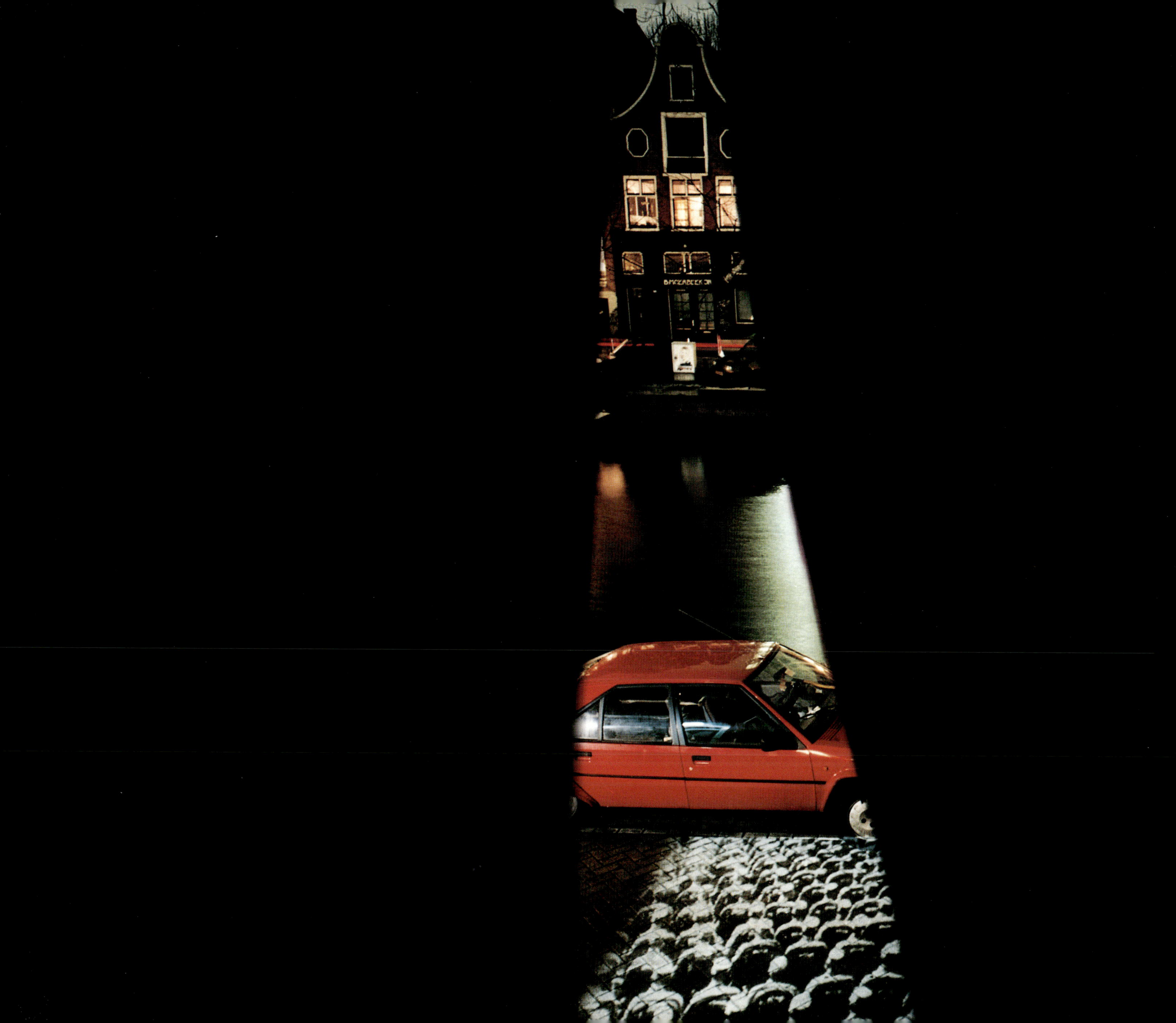

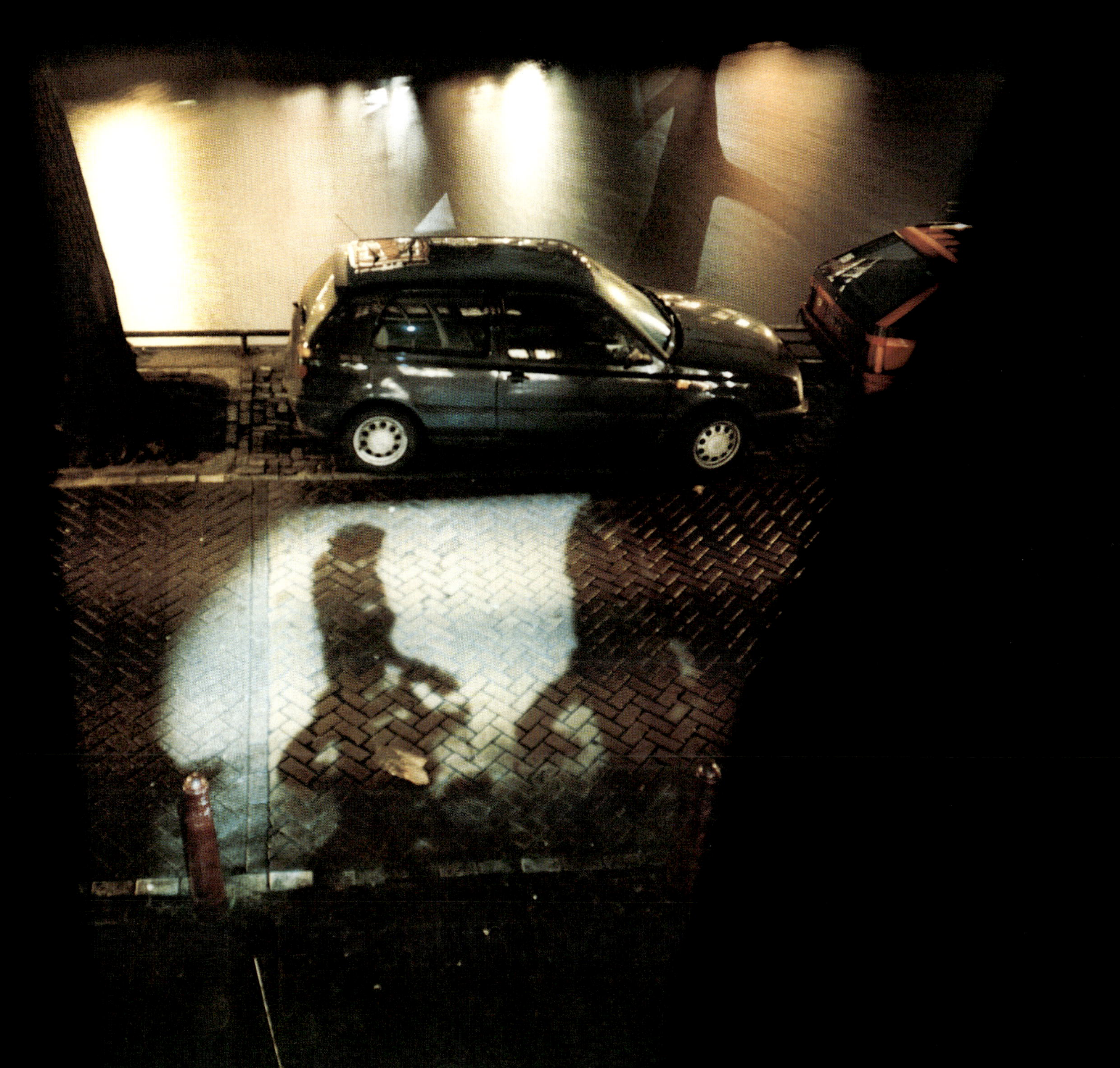

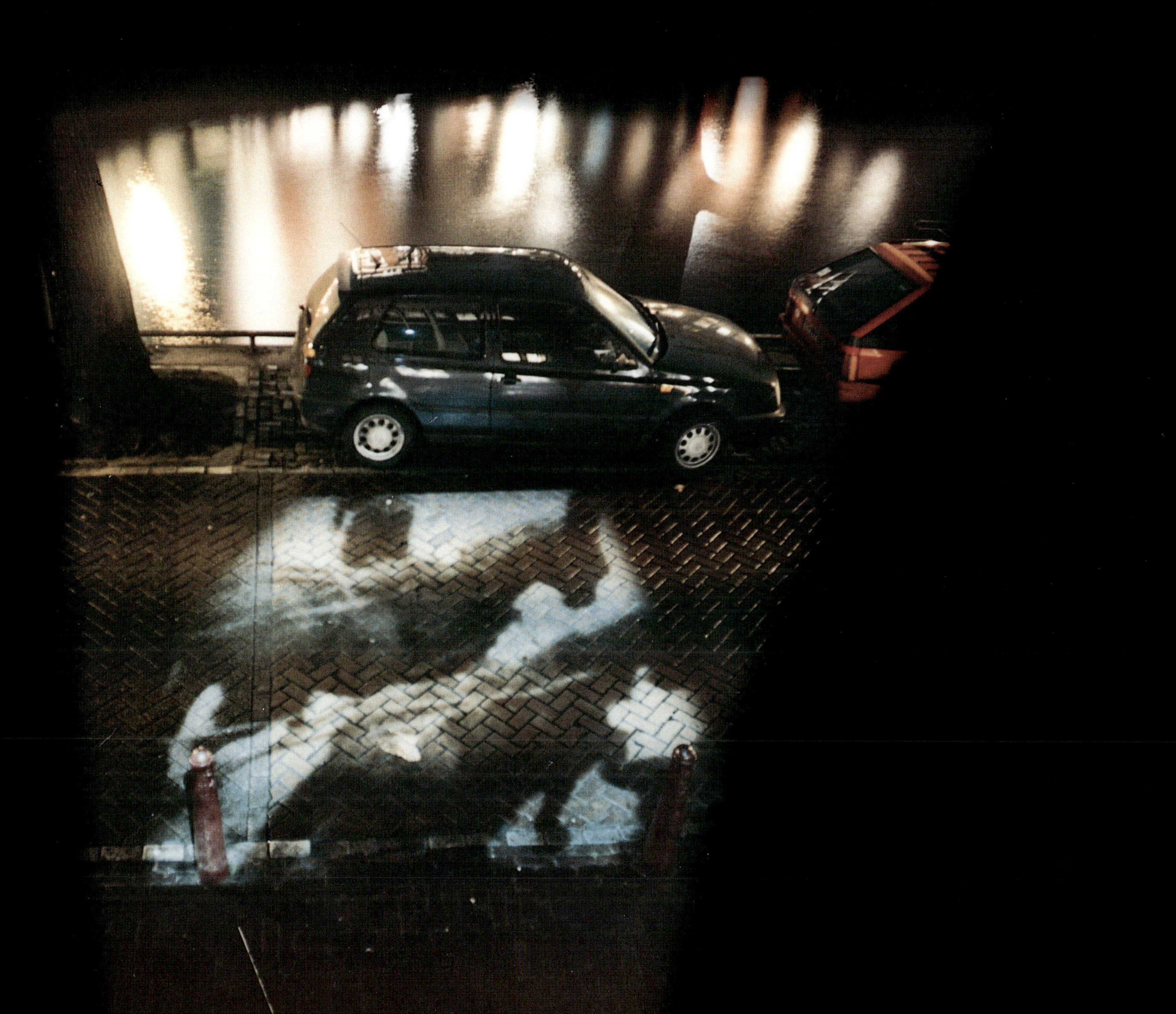

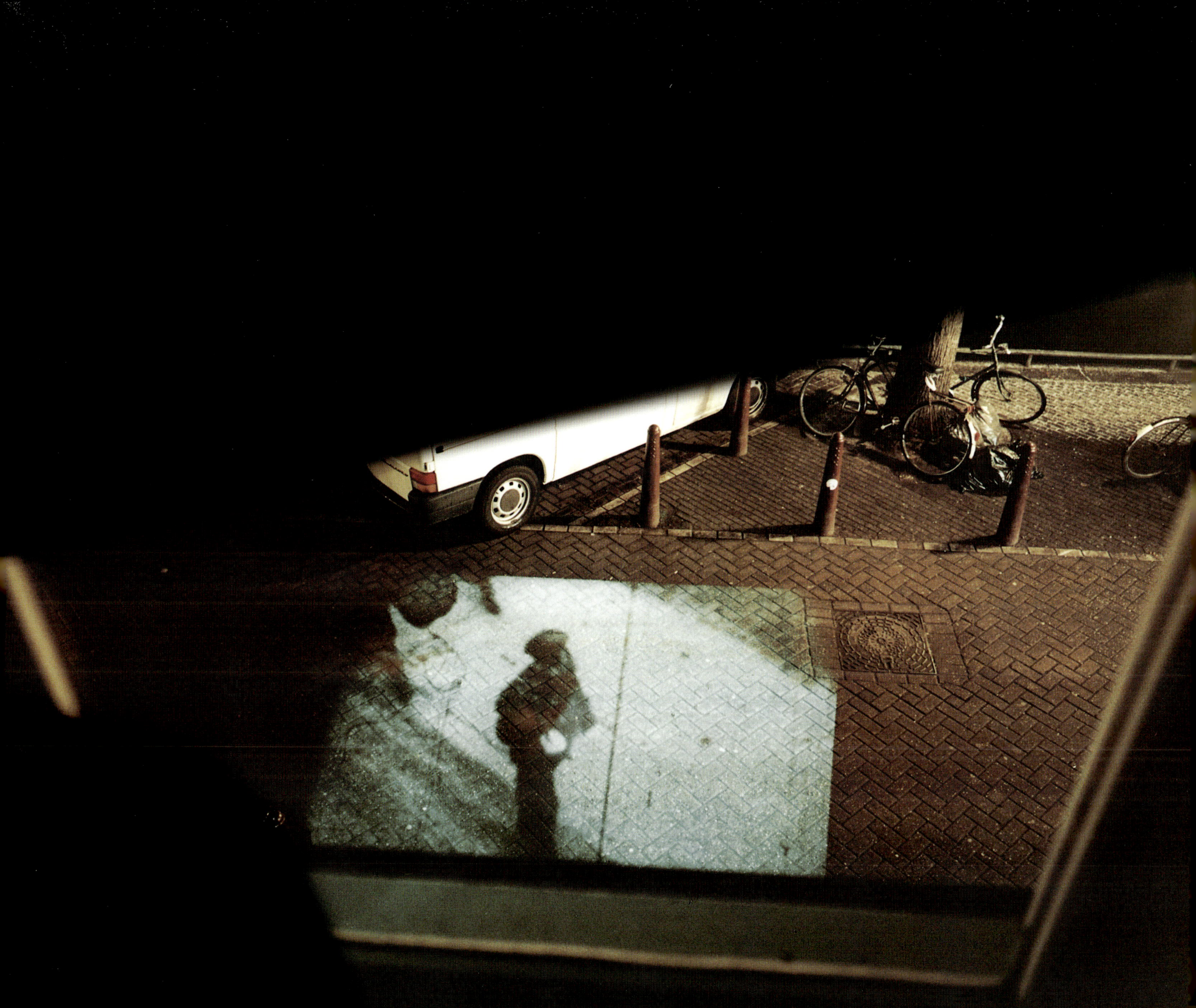

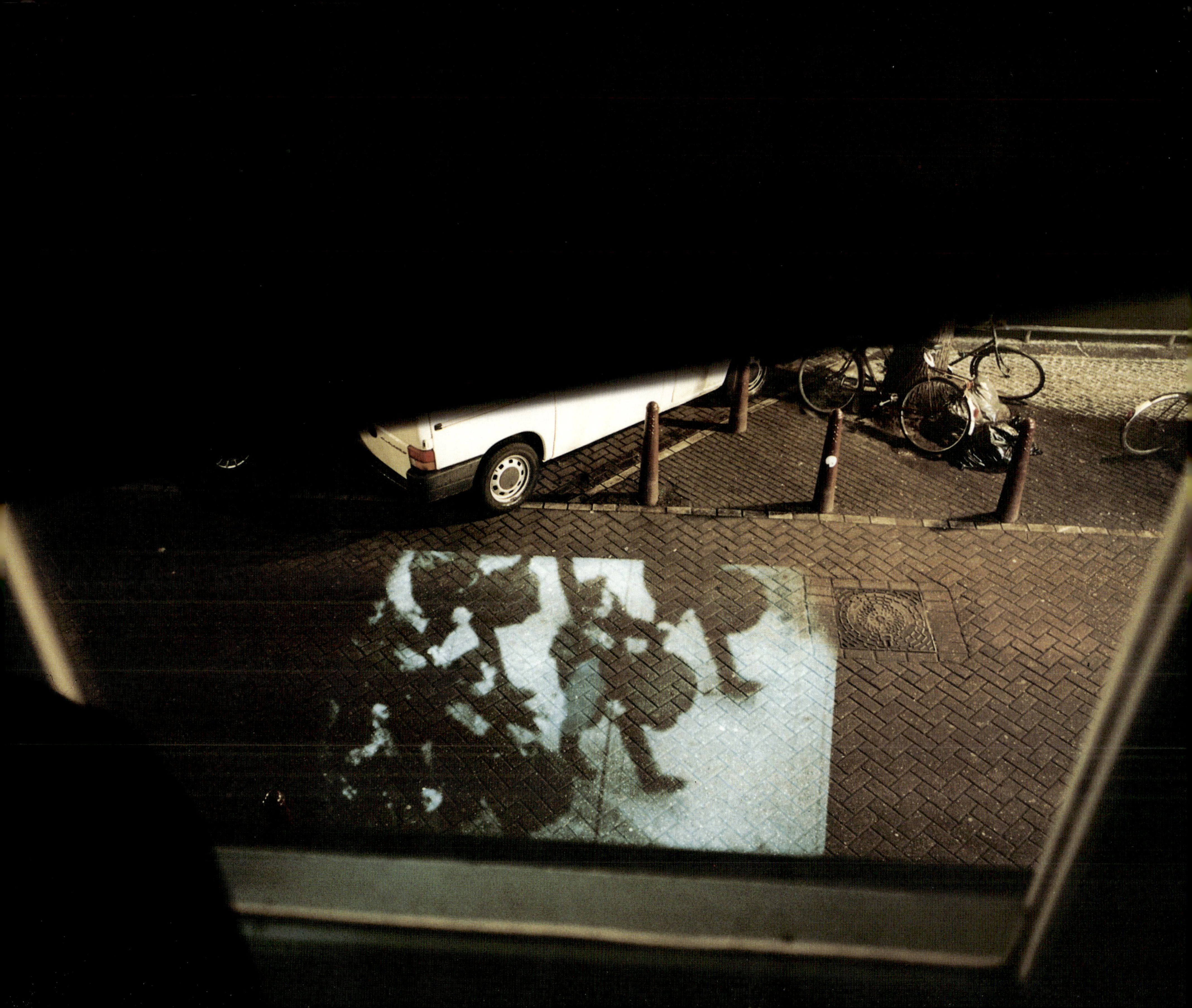

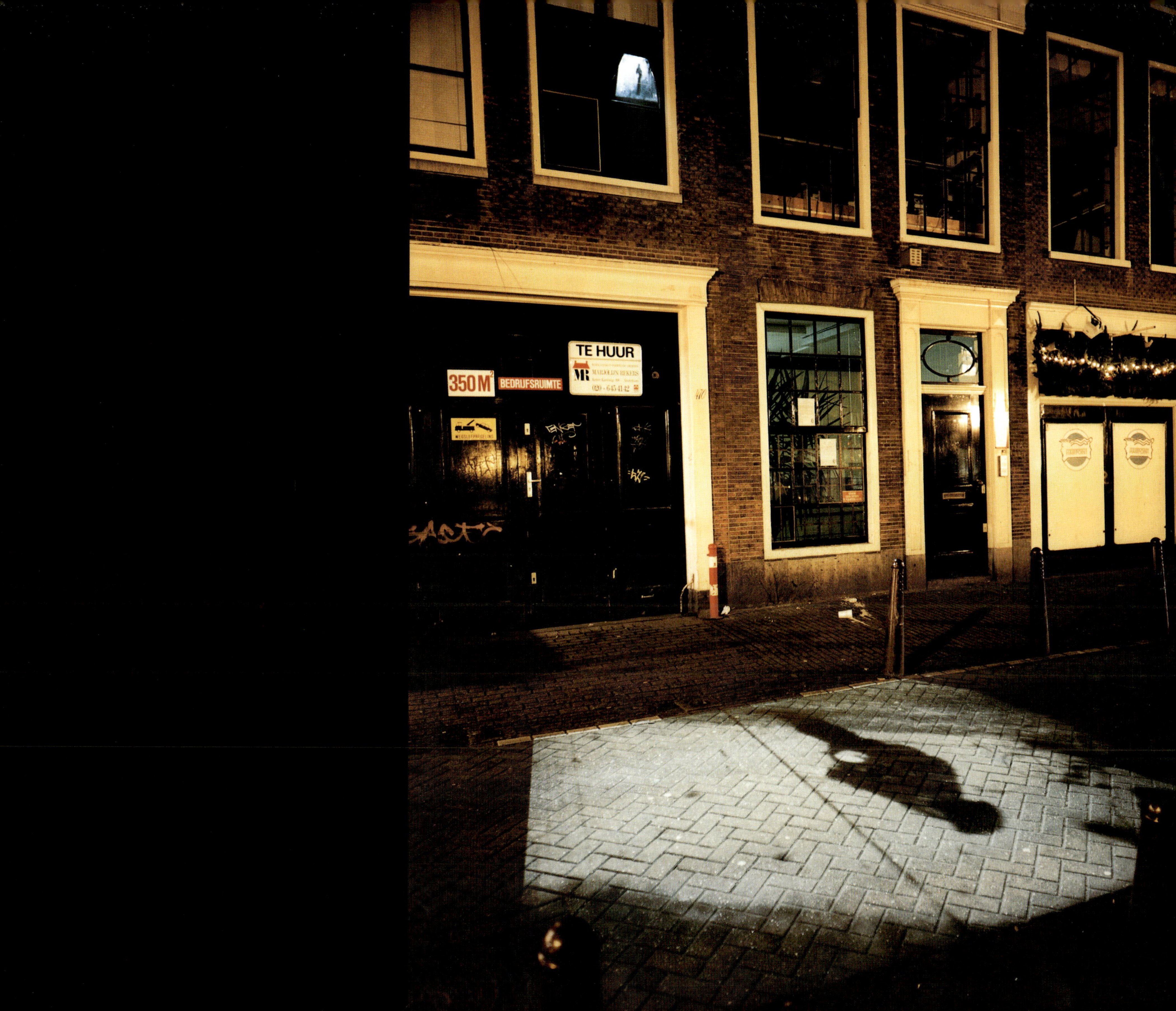

350 M²
BEDRIJFSRUIMTE
TE HUUR
MR
020 - 645 41 42

BRICK BY BRICK
November, 1995

Slide projections of household items at main entrance to *Art Cologne*, Cologne Fair Building (former warehouse and auction depot for household items confiscated from Jews and others during the war), Cologne, Germany

Realized in collaboration with Mathias Maile
based on a concept by Shimon Attie
organized by the Cologne *Kunstverein*

Brick by Brick took place within the context of one of Europe's most important commercial art events: *Art Cologne*. In an oddity of history, the art fair opens every year on the anniversary of *Reichskristallnacht*, in the Cologne Fair Building, a building with a dark and buried past. During Nazi terror, the Fair Building was used as a slave labor camp and deportation site for Cologne's Jews, Gypsies, and other persecuted individuals. The halls of the fair building also served as a warehouse for confiscated furniture and other household items belonging to Jews and others who were deported or forced to emigrate. These items were auctioned to members of the Nazi party whose houses suffered damage from allied bombing raids. During *Art Cologne*, images of furniture and other household items commonly found in middle class German-Jewish (and other) homes of the late 1930's and early 40's were slide projected onto the 9 brick columns leading up to the main entrance and exit of the fair building and *Art Cologne*.

Many of these same items can still be found in German households today as "antiques". *Brick by Brick* took place November 10–12, 1995.

59 Installation Shot

60 On column in foreground: *Sewing Machine, ca. 1910*

63 On column in foreground: *Chair, ca. 1910*

64 On column in foreground: *Lamp, 1920*

67 On column in foreground: *Commode (Gründerzeit), ca. 1880*

68 On column in foreground: *Menorah (Bauhaus), ca. 1930*

70 On column in foreground: *Chest (Bauhaus), ca. 1925*

73 On column in foreground: *Carrying bag, ca. 1940*

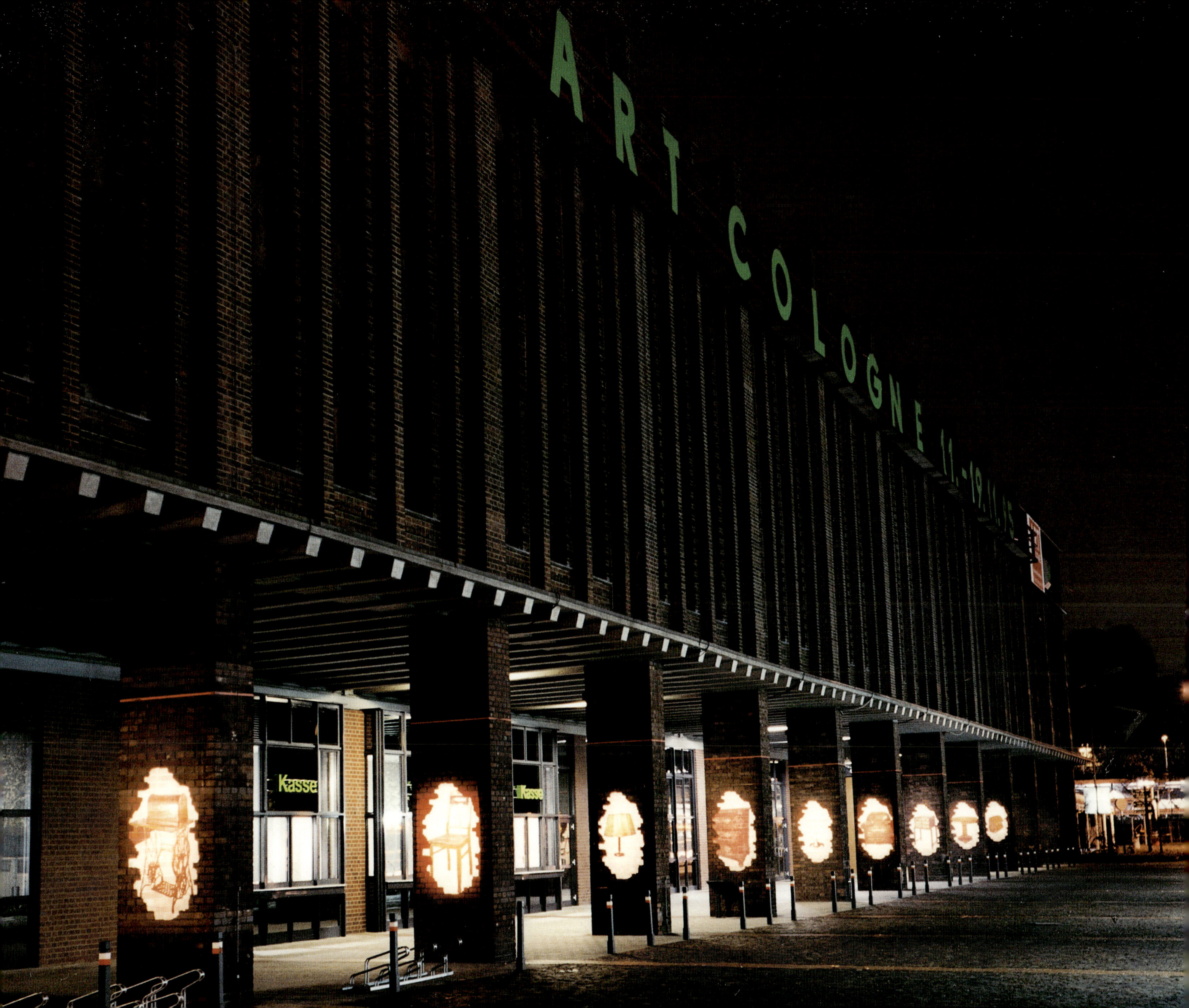
ART COLOGNE 11.–19.11.95
Kasse
Kasse

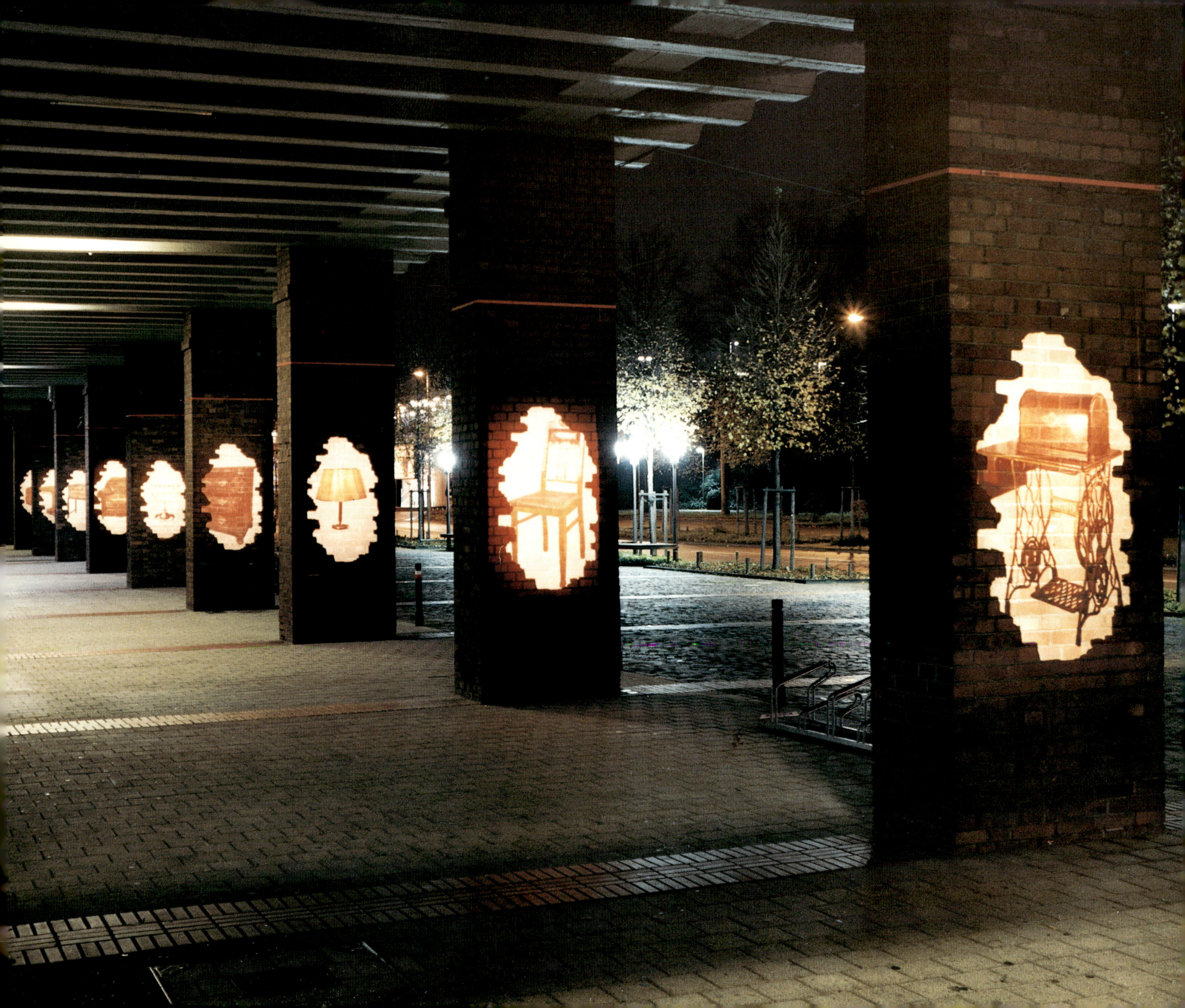

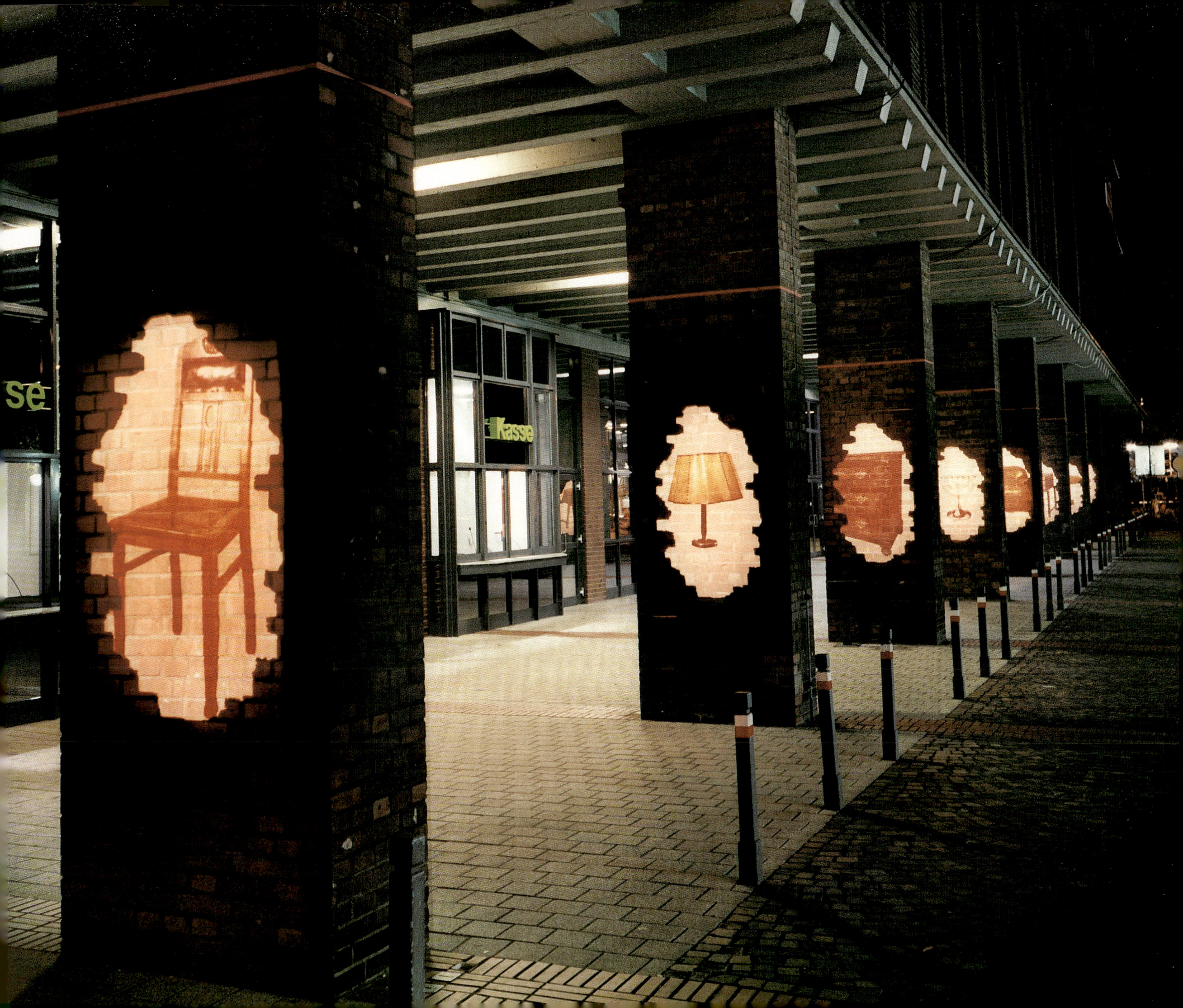
Kasse

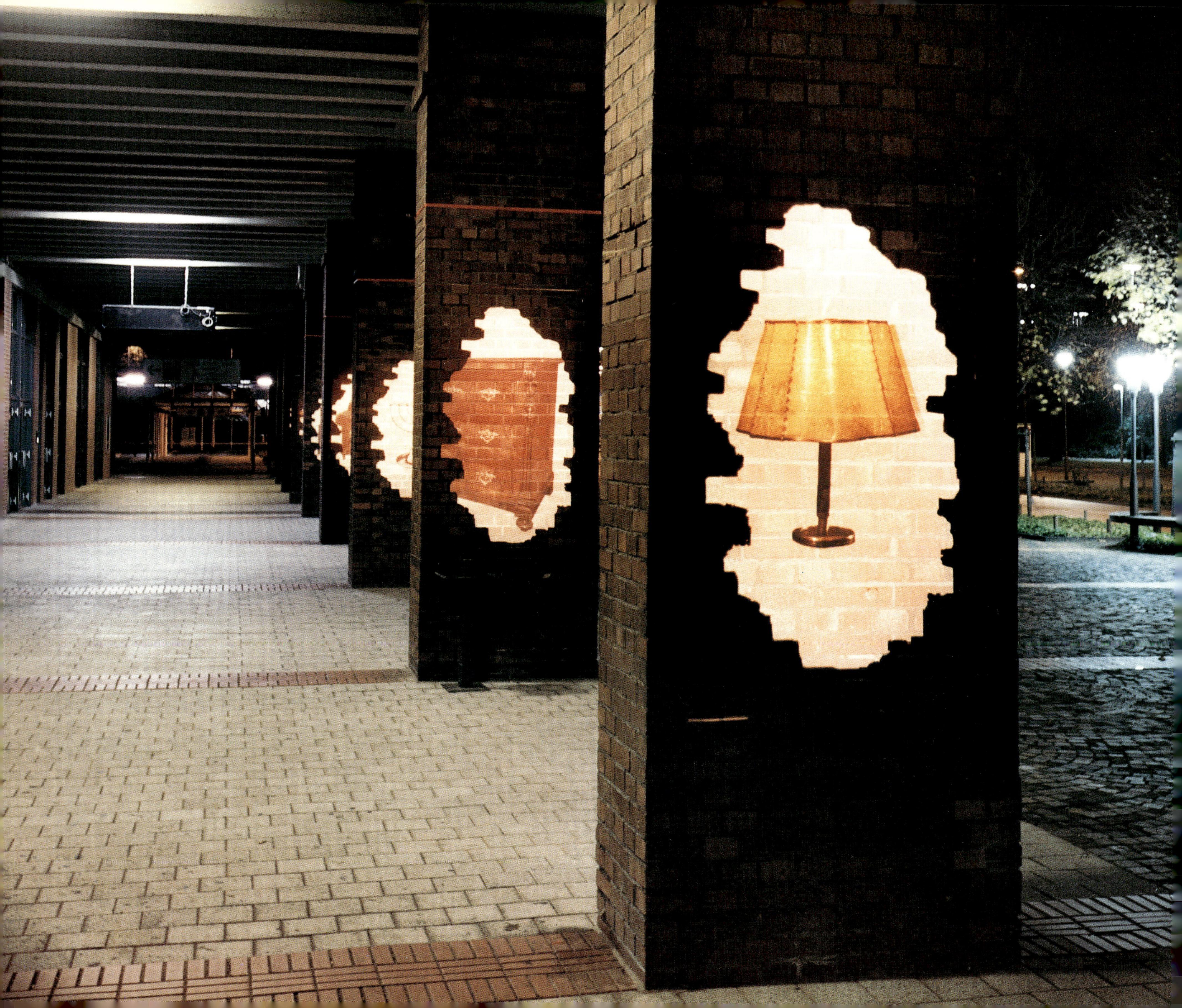

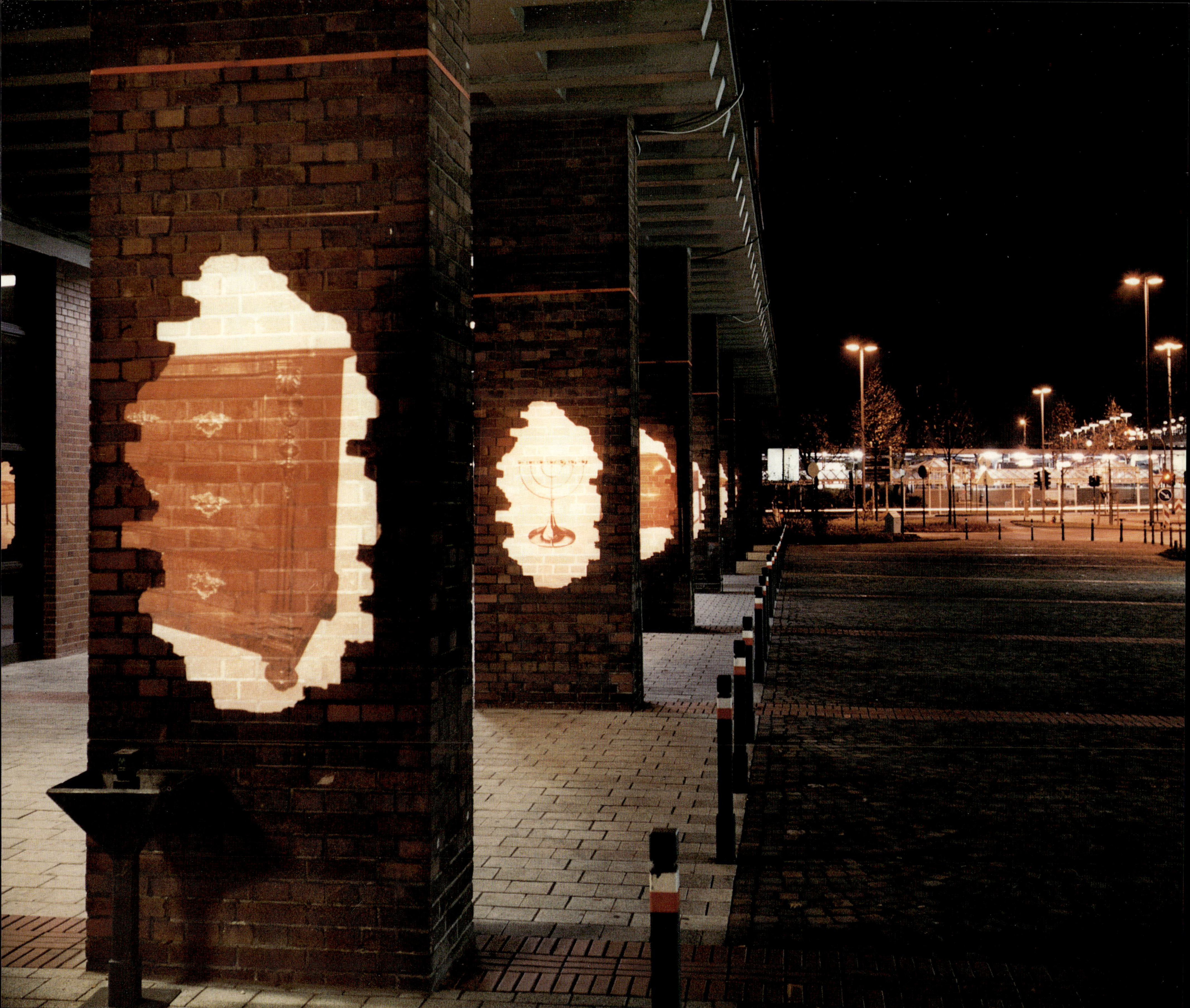

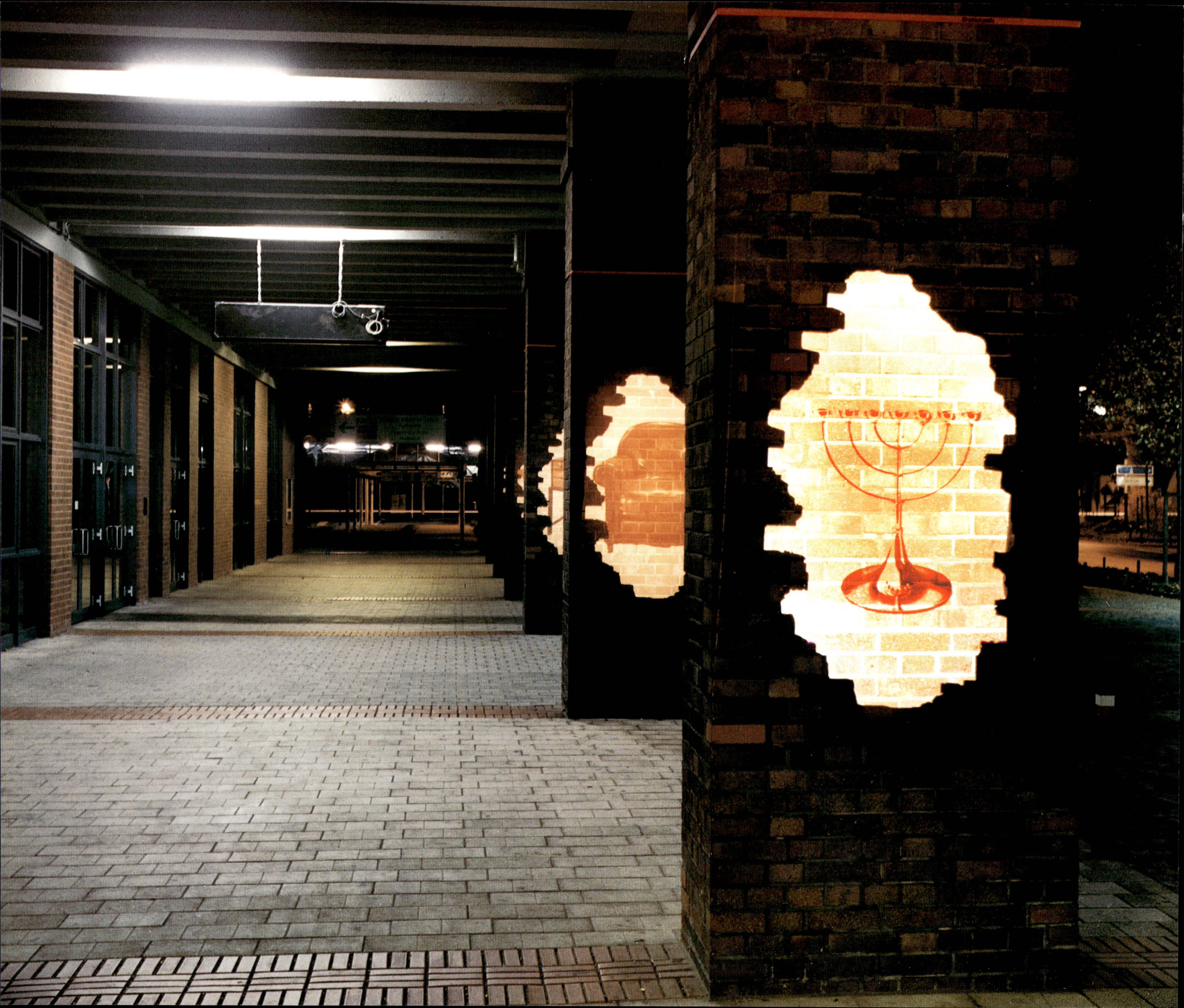

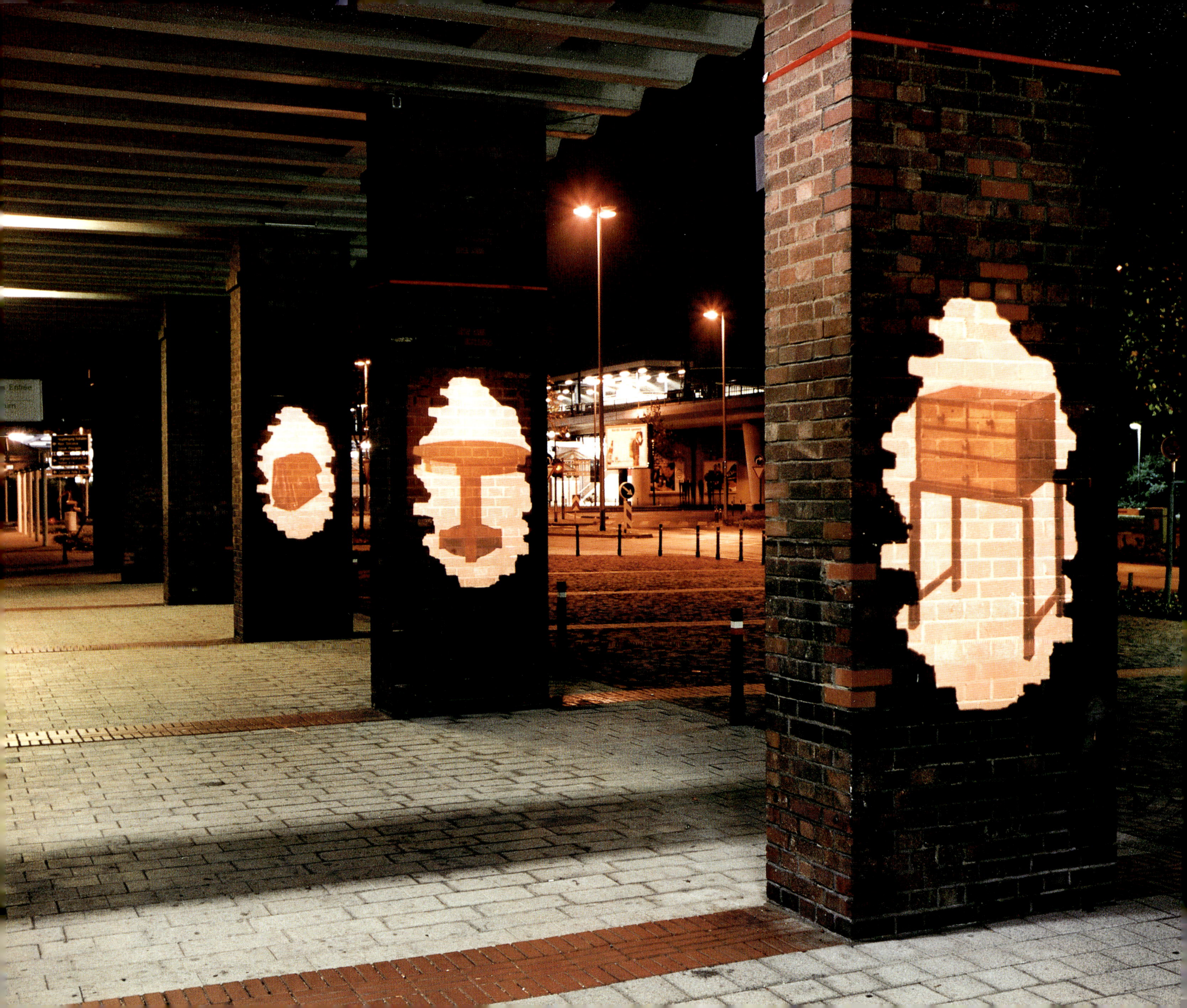

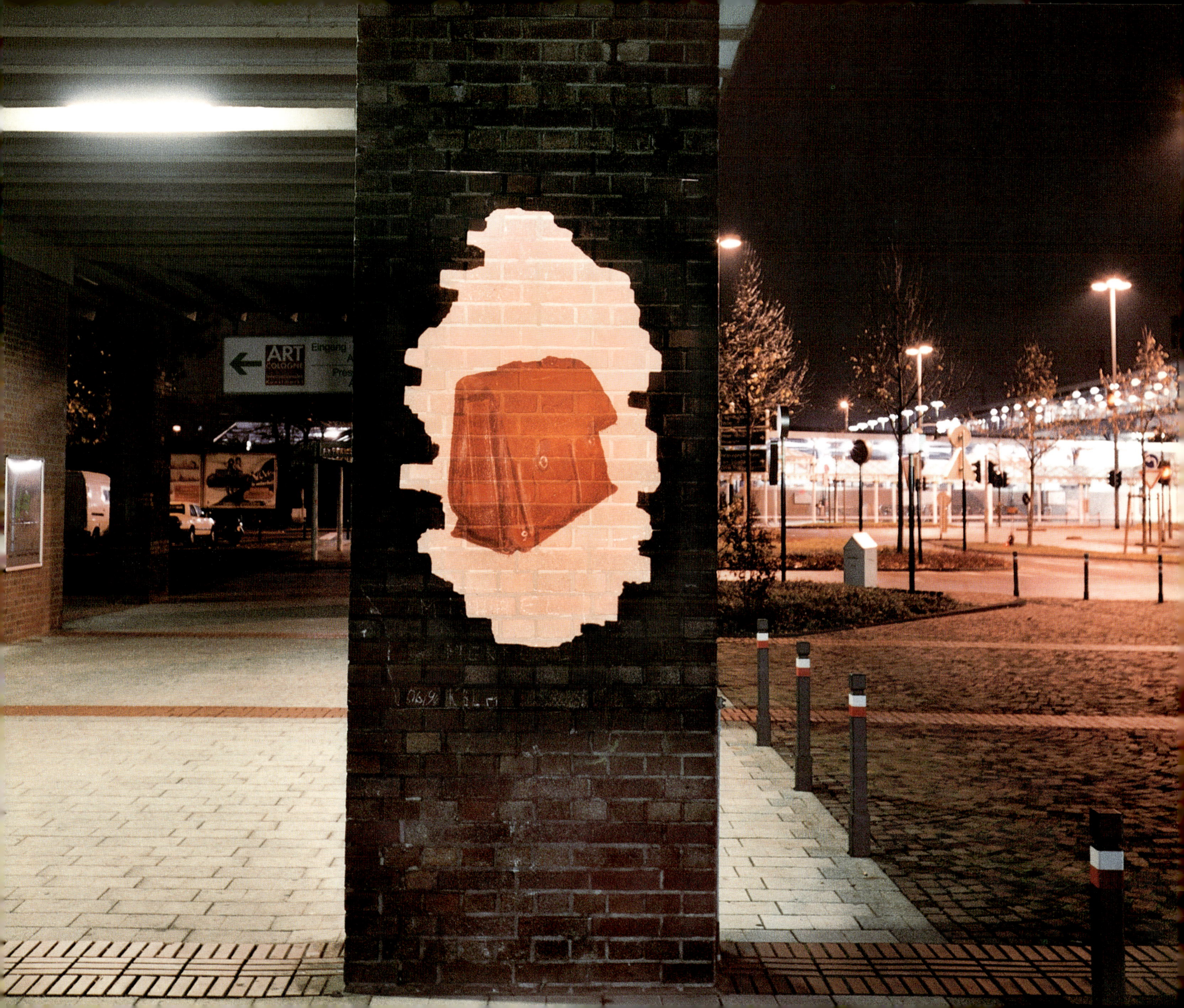
ART
COLOGNE
Eingang

TRAINS
November, 1993

76 Former persecuted Dresden Jewish citizen

77 Former persecuted Dresden Jewish citizen

78 Yiddish newspaper The Future, Nov. 1923 issue

79 Former persecuted Dresden Jewish citizen

Slide projections at the Central Train Station, Dresden, Germany

Realized in collaboration with Mathias Maile based on a concept by Shimon Attie

T*rains* took place in Dresden's central train station. Portrait photographs of former Jewish citizens of Dresden who had been persecuted during national socialism were slide projected onto trains, tracks, and walls of the central station.
Additionally, the front page of a Yiddish newspaper from 1923, entitled *The Future*, was projected onto the floor of the station near the main information display boards. This served to frame Germany's history in light of the troubling recent rise of racist and xenophobic attacks against foreigners which have swept the country in recent years.
The portrait photographs used for the project were gathered from Dresden's tiny Jewish community today. Members of the community volunteered photographs of relatives and friends from family photo albums.
Trains opened on November 9, 1993 and ran for approximately 2 weeks.

TRAINS · DRESDEN · GERMANY

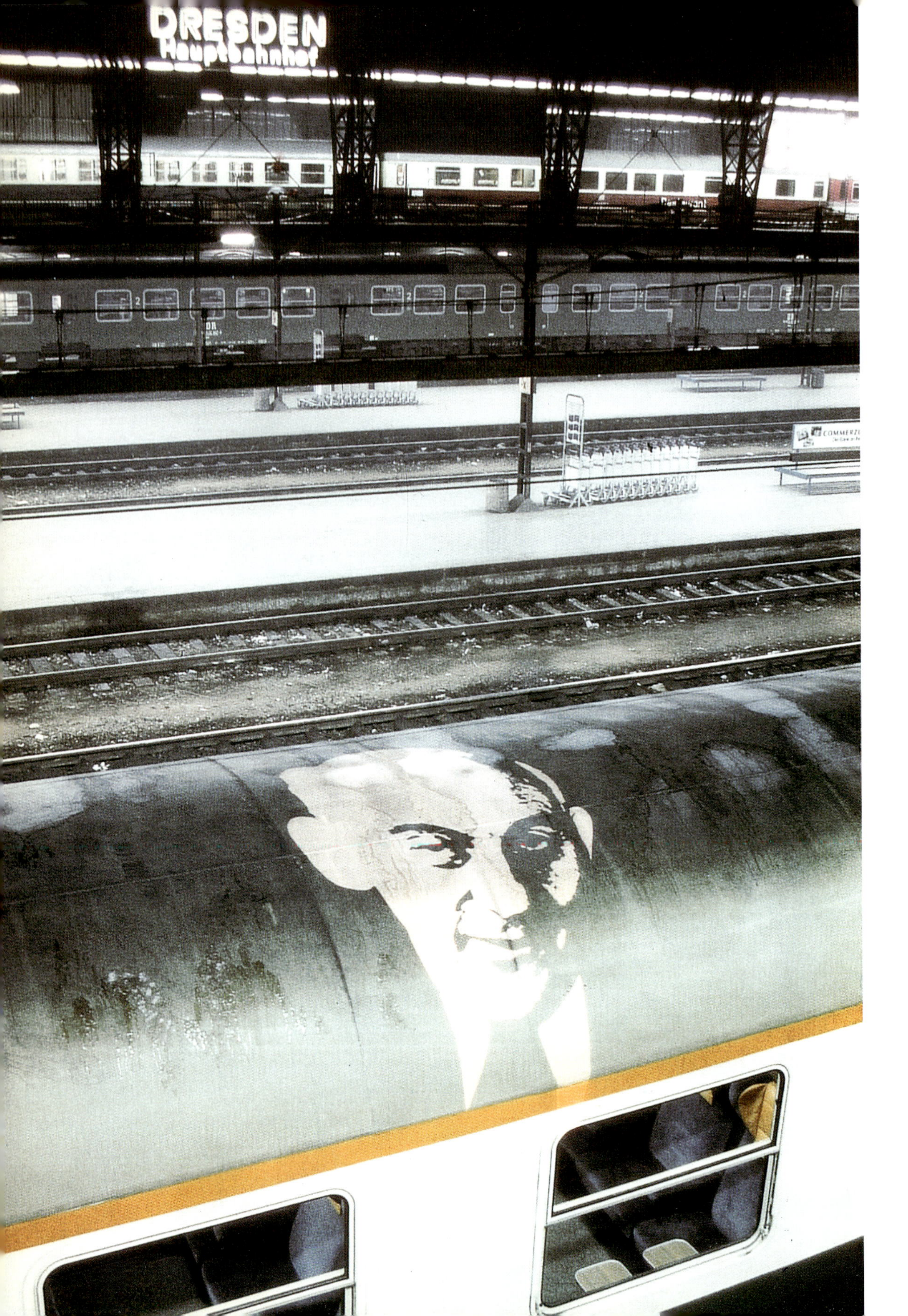
DRESDEN
Hauptbahnhof

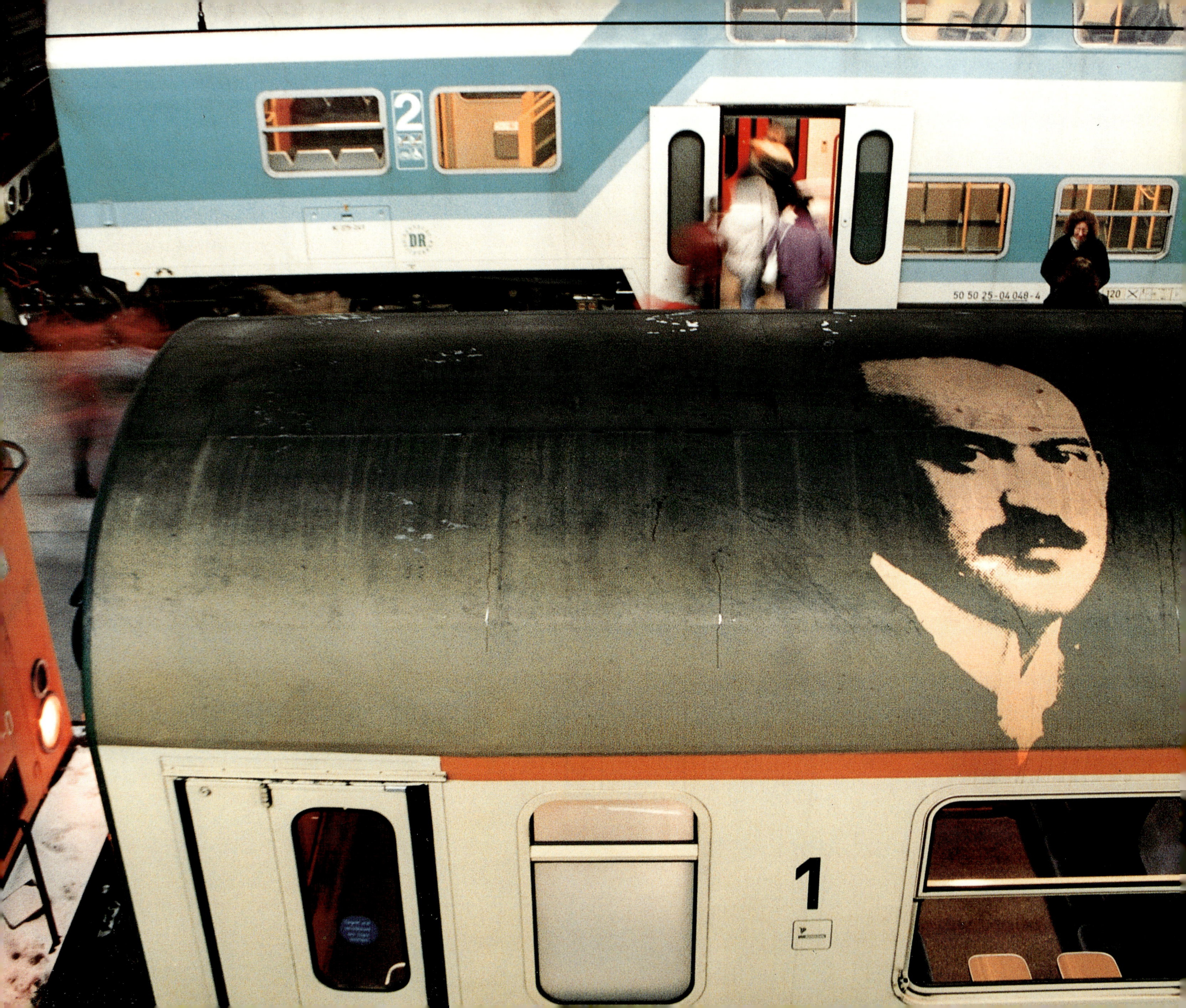
2
DR
50 50 25-04 048-4
1

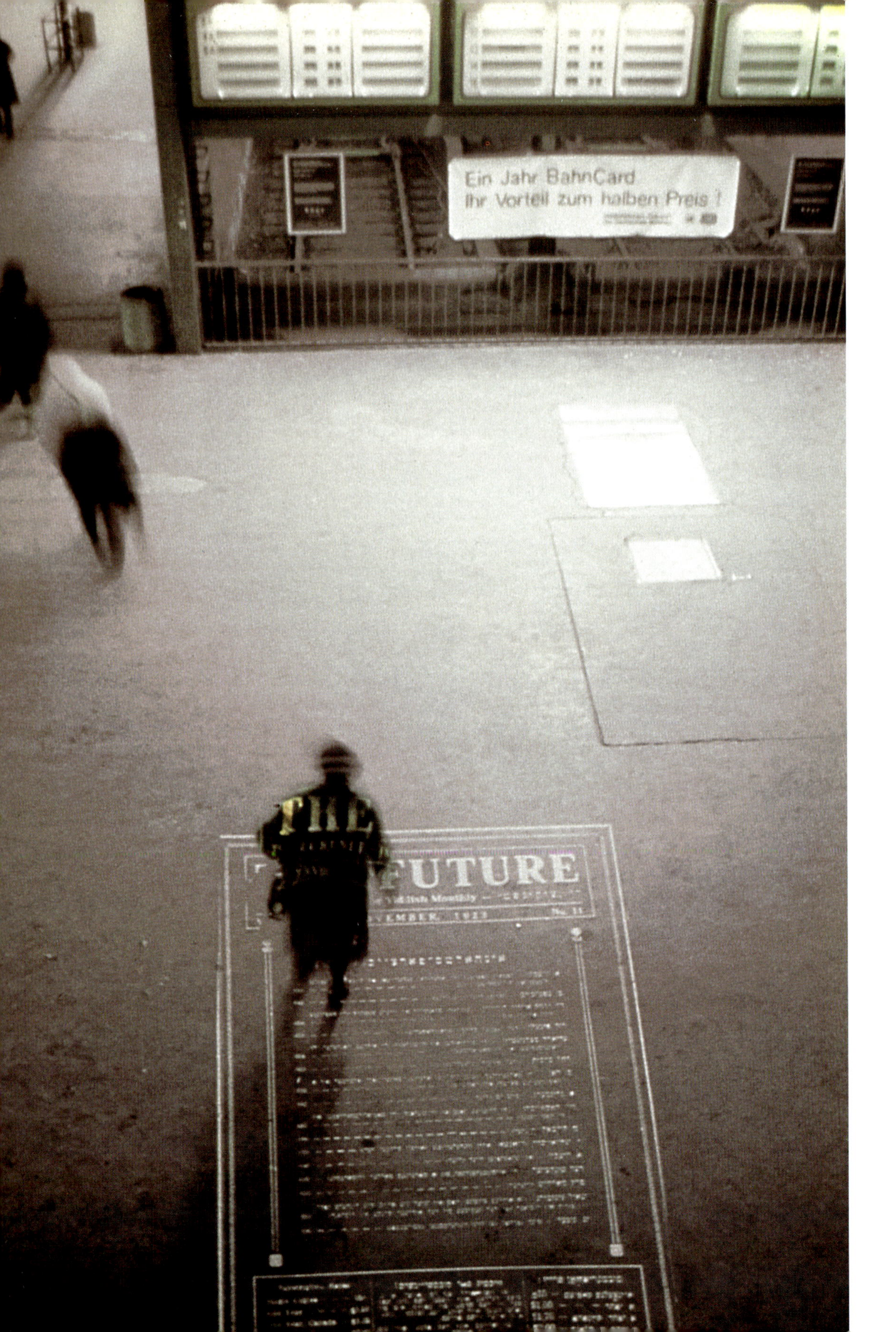
Ein Jahr BahnCard
Ihr Vorteil zum halben Preis !
FUTURE

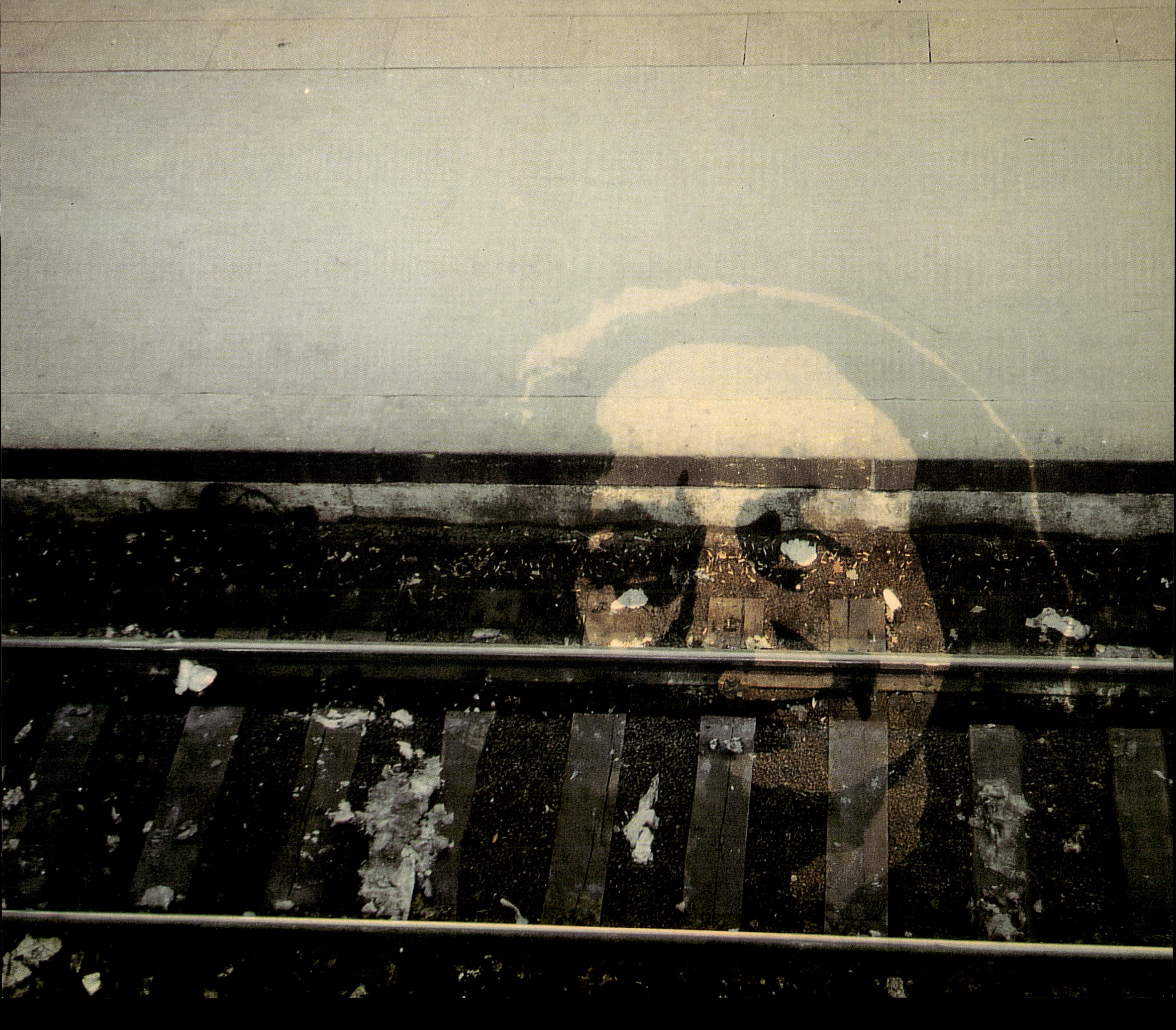

THE WALK OF FAME
June – July, 1996

83 I. Izraelowicz

84 J. H. Borenstein

85 H. Blumantricht

86 A. Auerbach

87 H. R. Feldmann

88 Installation shot. In foreground: *J. Rosenberg*

89 Installation shot. In foreground: *M. L. Hellmann*

91 Installation shot

Twenty-four 80 x 80 cm simulated terrazzo stars installed on square in front of the Old Synagogue (near sites used for the filming of *Schindler's List*), Szeroka Street, Krakow, Poland

Organized and produced by the Judaica Foundation-Center for Jewish Culture and the Goethe Institute, Krakow

Today in Krakow, as elsewhere, our awareness and understanding of the history of the Second World War is steadily being displaced and determined by contemporary cinema. The result has been a confusion and inversion between actual history and history-as-created-for-the-movies. On the Szeroka Street for example, through the use of film sets, a mock-up version of the Krakow Ghetto erected by the Nazis was created for the filming of Steven Spielberg's *Schindler's List*, although the actual location was in the Podgorze district of Krakow.

As we lose a direct and unmediated relationship with this history, with a motion picture camera and screen now intervening, authentic historical sites, events and individuals are now in open competition with their celluloid copies in determining our understanding of history. As actual history becomes conflated with cinematic fiction, it becomes more and more difficult to distinguish between the two. Local residents and tourists to Krakow must now choose between guided tours to authentic historical sites and guided tours "Retracing the Filming of *Schindler's List*".

Inspired by Hollywood Boulevard's *Walk of Fame* in Los Angeles, for this project the square in front of the Old Synagogue on Szeroka Street was lined with twenty-four simulated 5-pointed terrazzo stars. The original version in Los Angeles is intended to publicly acknowledge and enshrine movie stars of exceptional talent and accomplishment by in-laying their names into the sidewalks of Hollywood Boulevard. The stars used in Krakow were based on the originals in Los Angeles, of nearly identical size, but were aesthetically altered to suit the site, which was in front of the Jewish Museum and former Old Synagogue. Instead of the names of movie stars, the names of actual persons who were on the real Schindler's List were substituted. Their first names were abbreviated to protect their true identities.

The Walk of Fame project was not directed towards the individuals who lived through these horrible events, nor towards the specifics of any one film or cinematic event. Rather, its intention was to highlight and critically reflect the larger problematic eclipsing of historical fact by cinematic fiction – a phenomenon through which what we see at the movies becomes confused and taken for the *real*.

The Walk of Fame project was realized with the technical assistance of Karlheinz Reimann. *The Walk of Fame* project took place June 23–July 7, 1996.

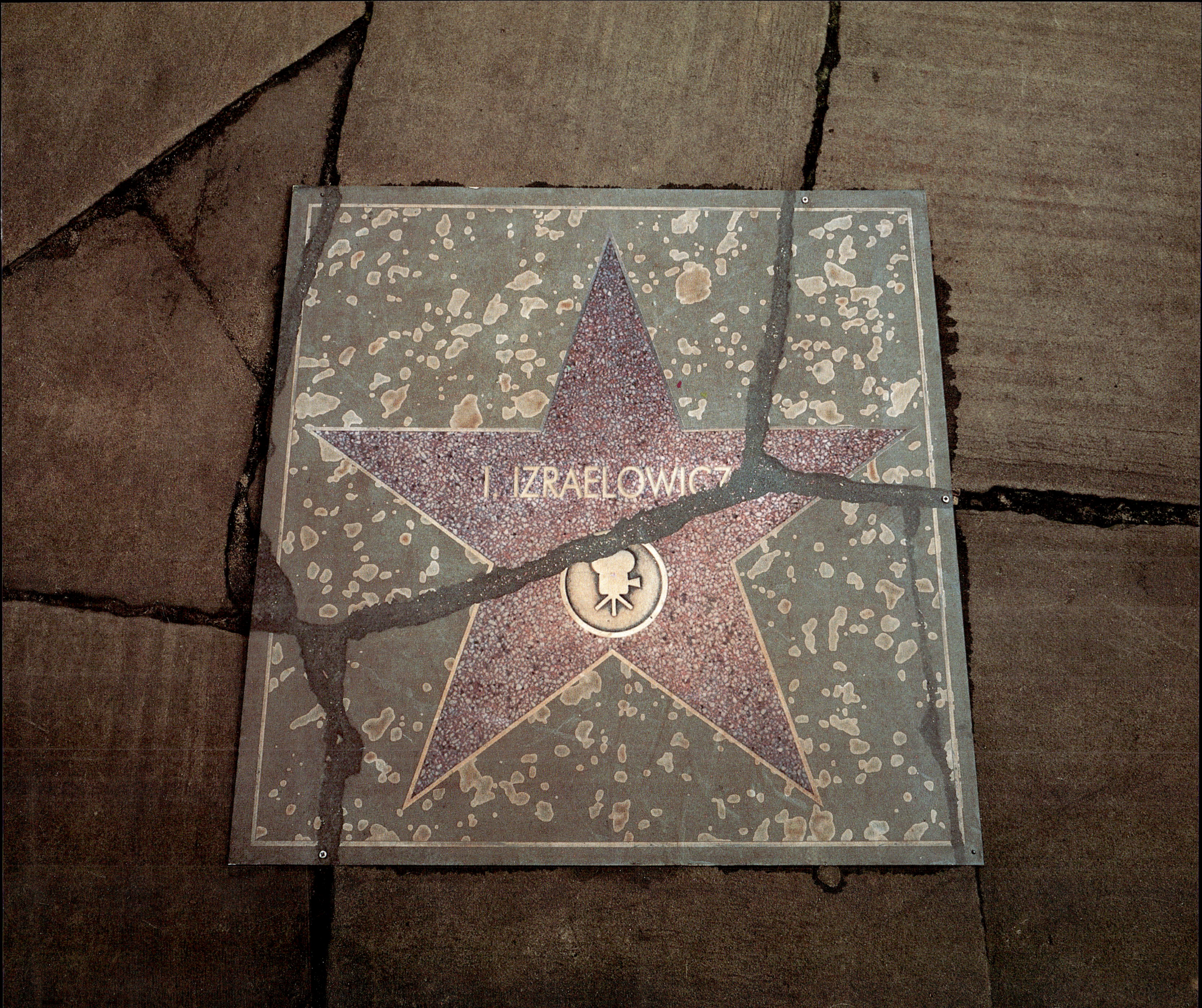
I. IZRAELOWICZ

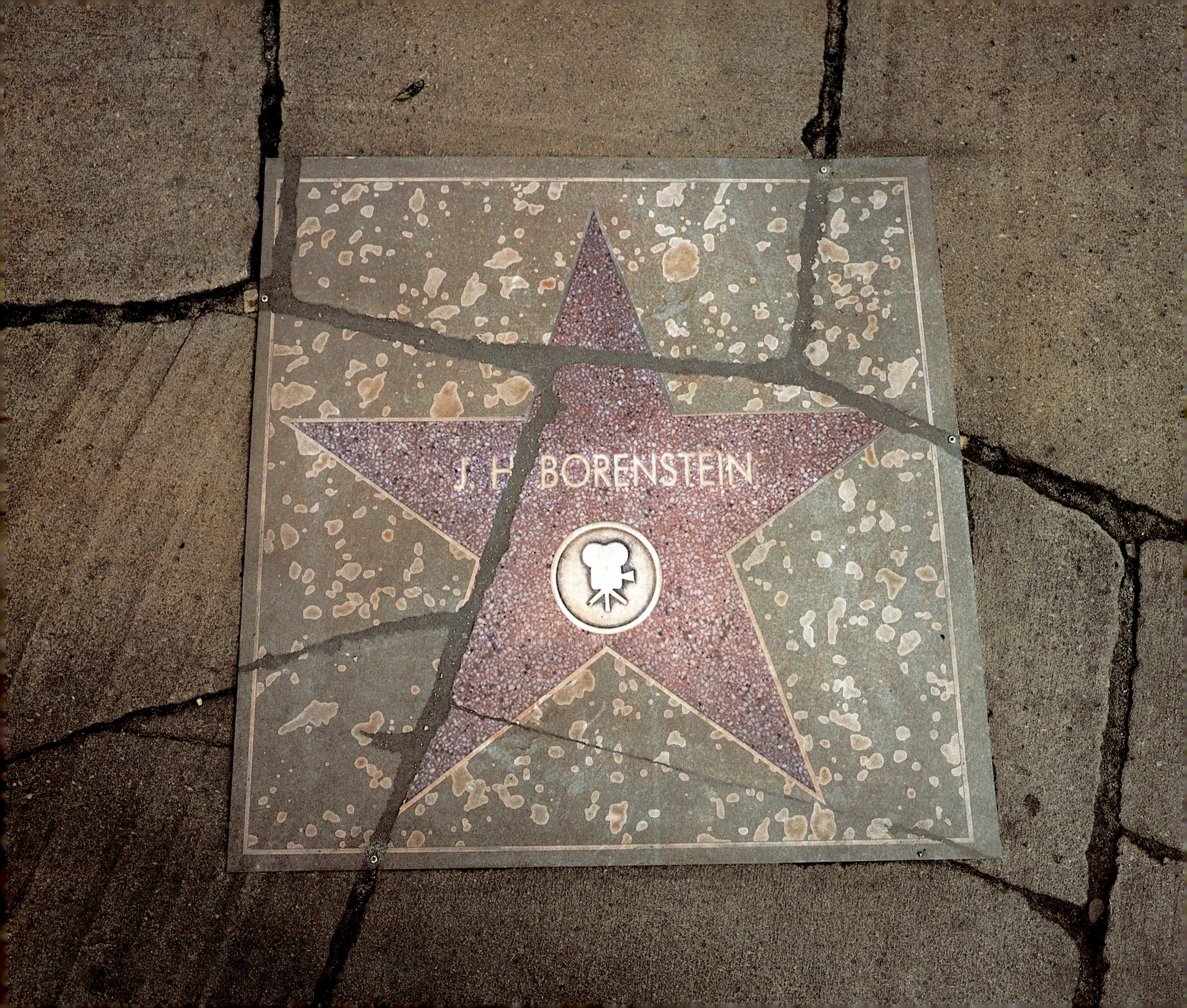
J. H BORENSTEIN

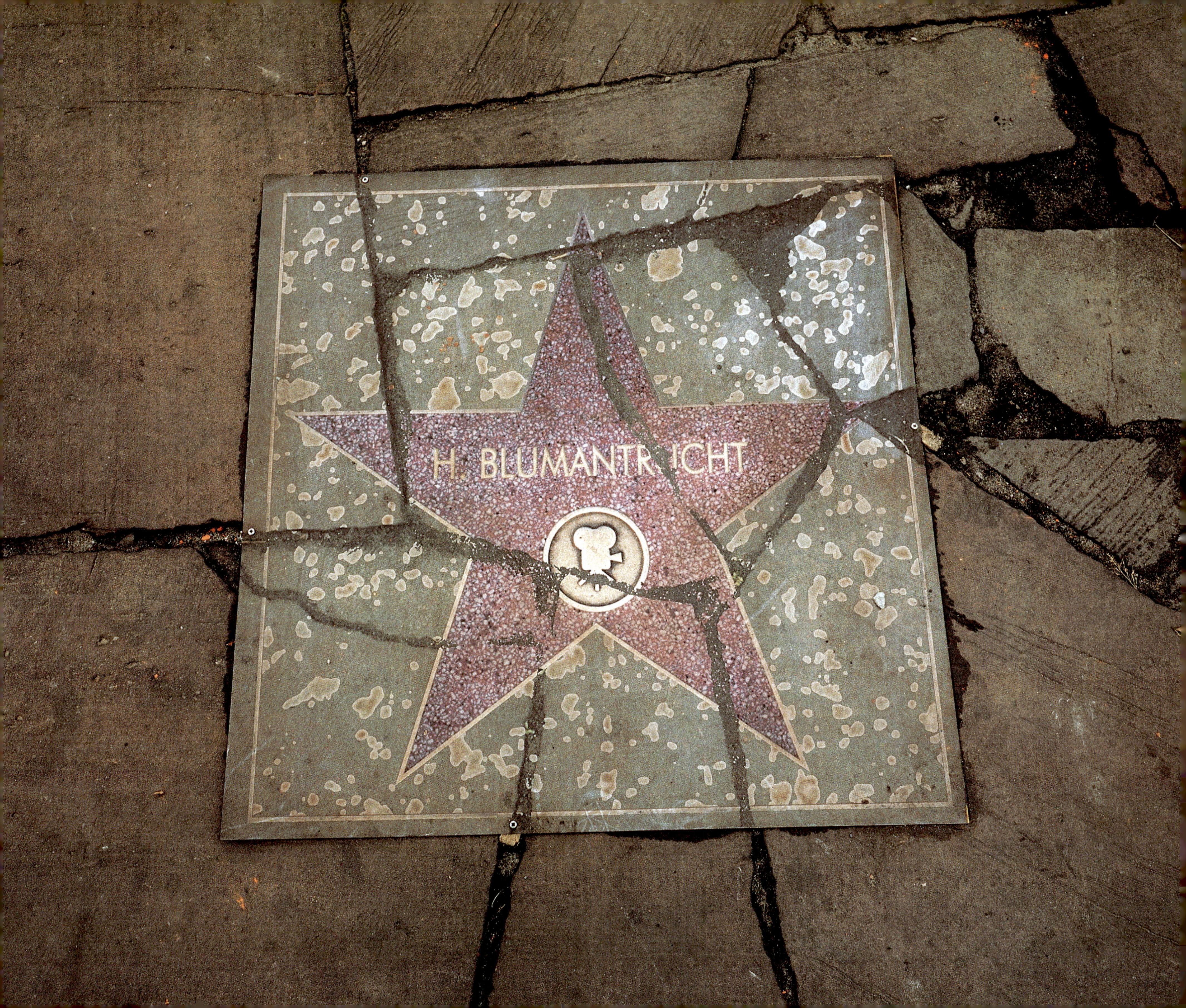
H. BLUMANTR ICHT

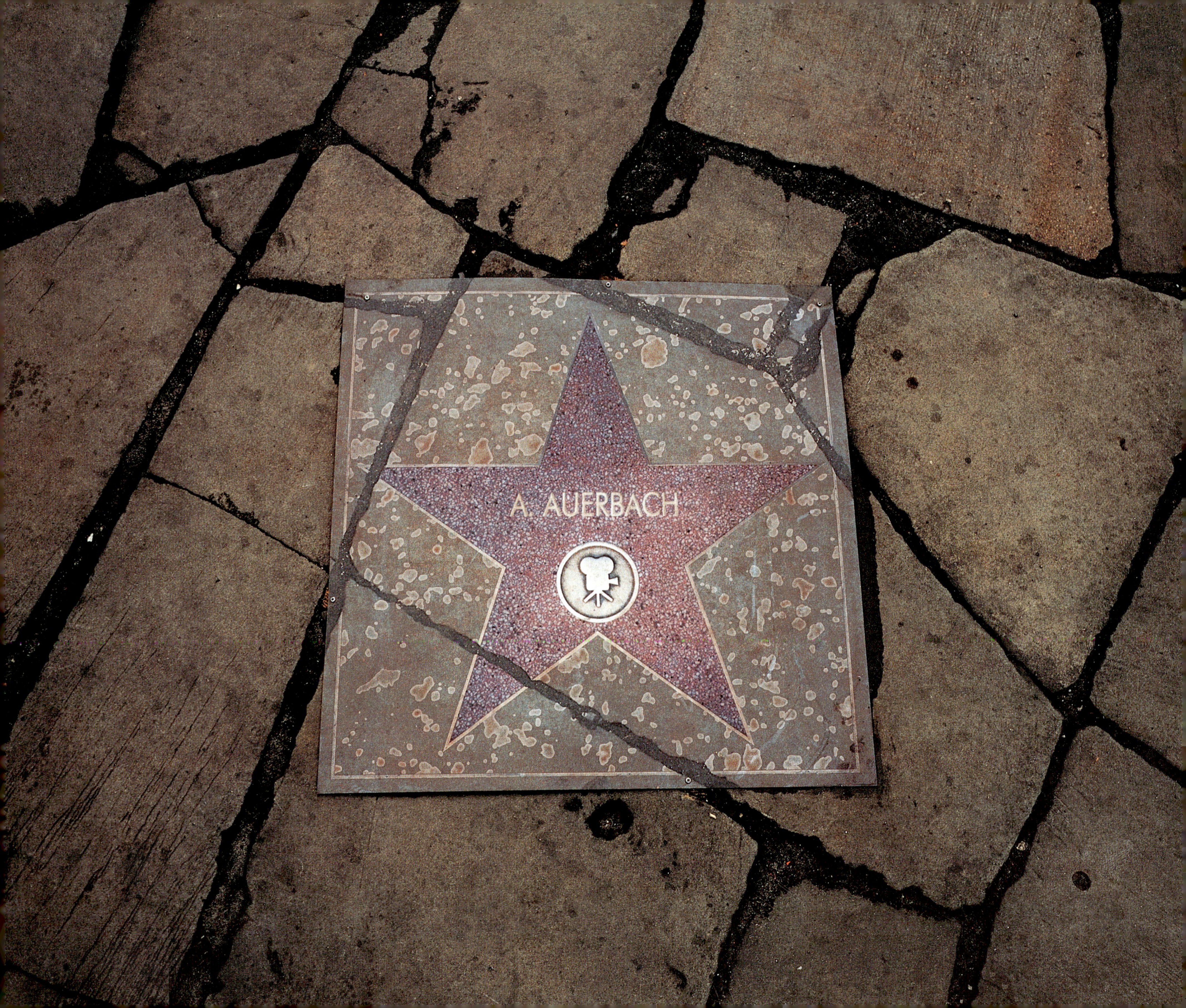
A. AUERBACH

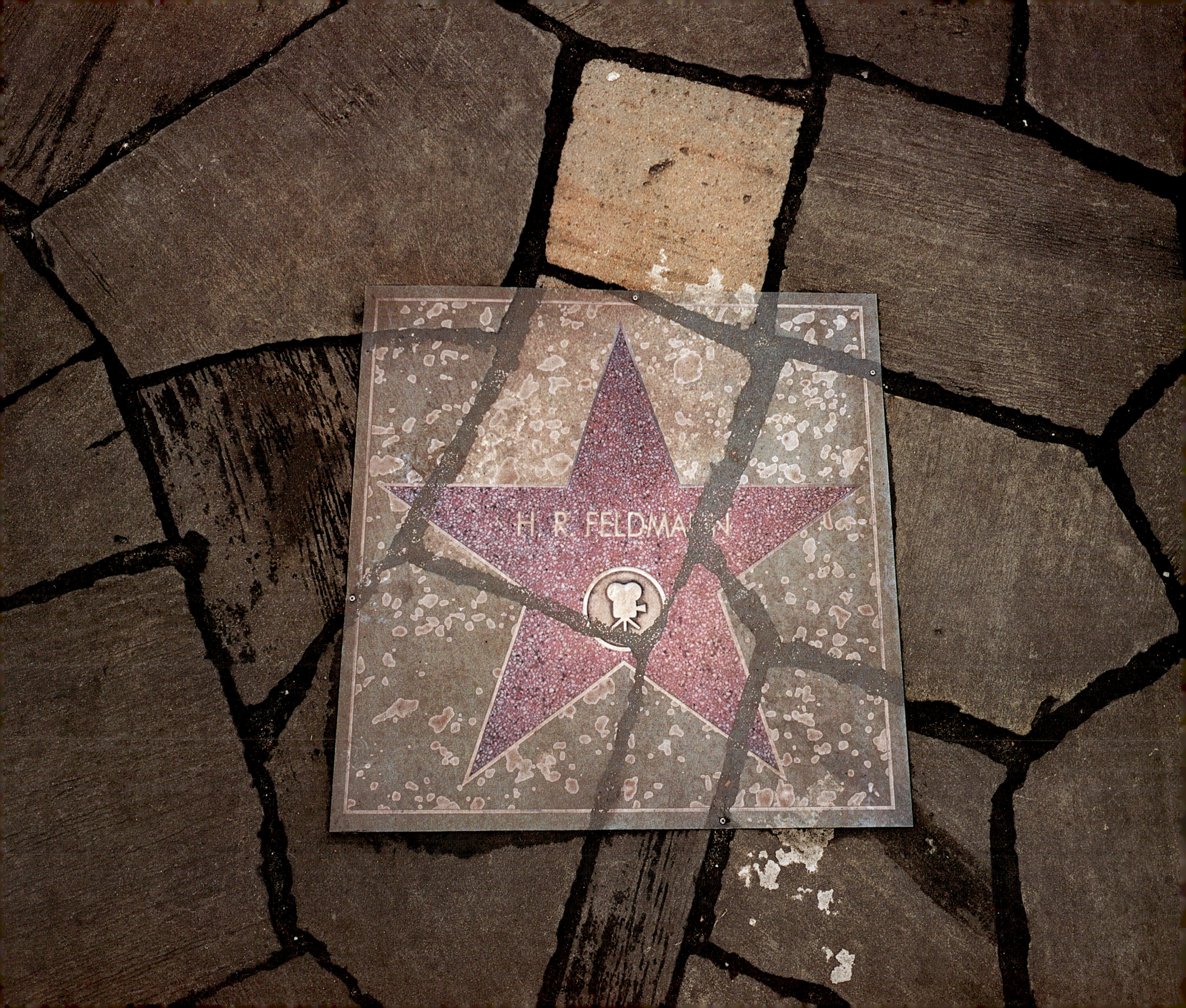
H. R. FELDMA N

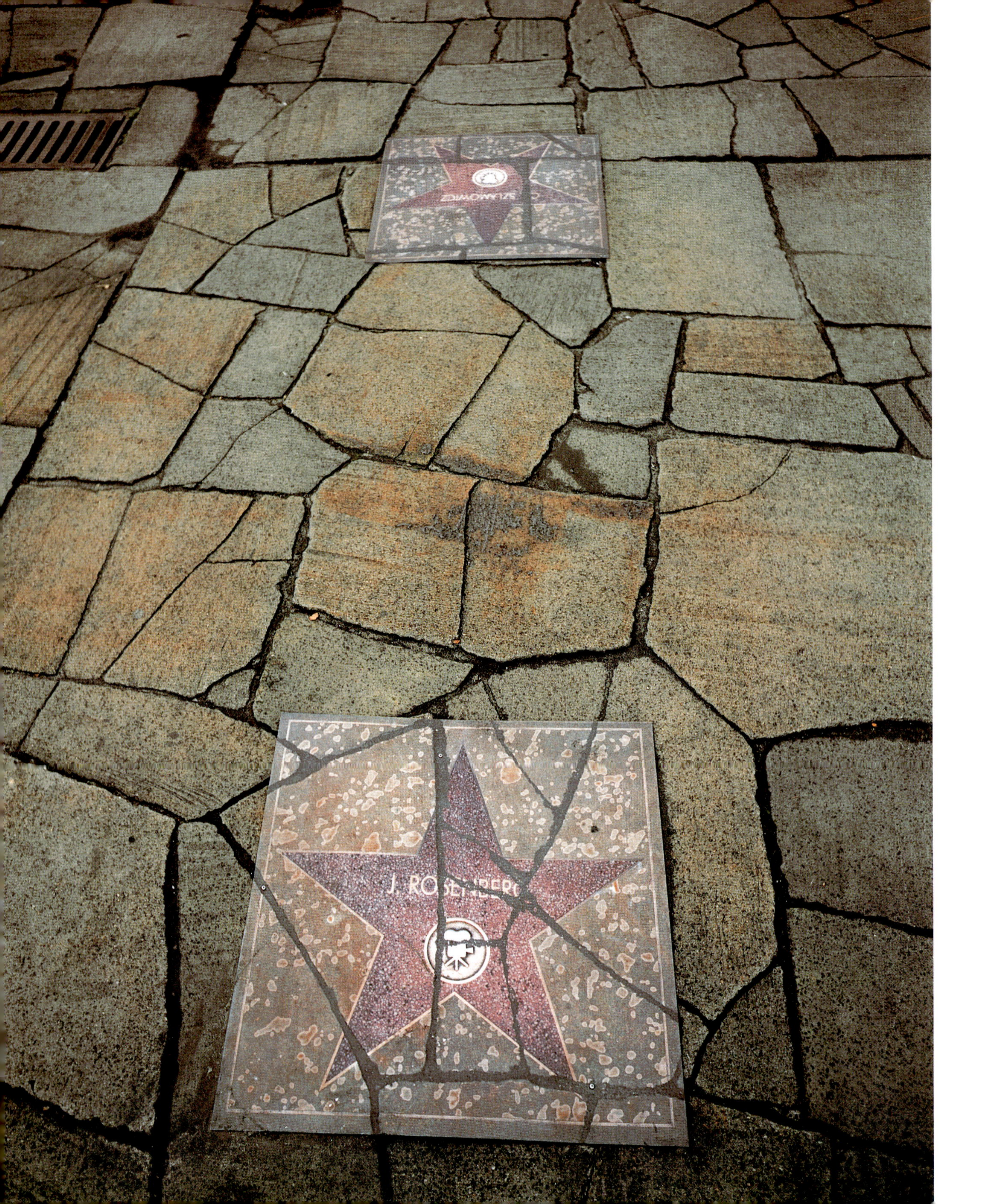

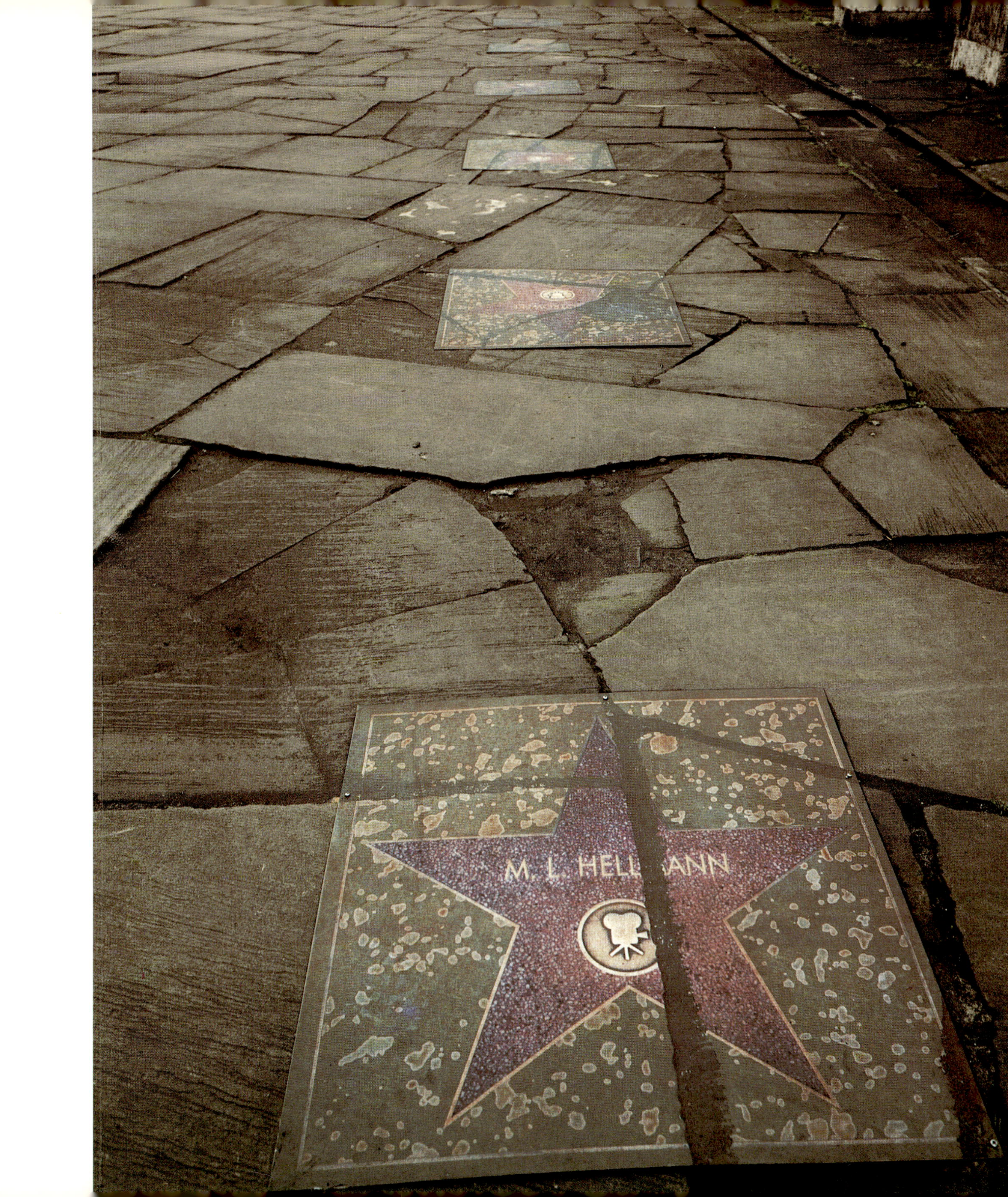

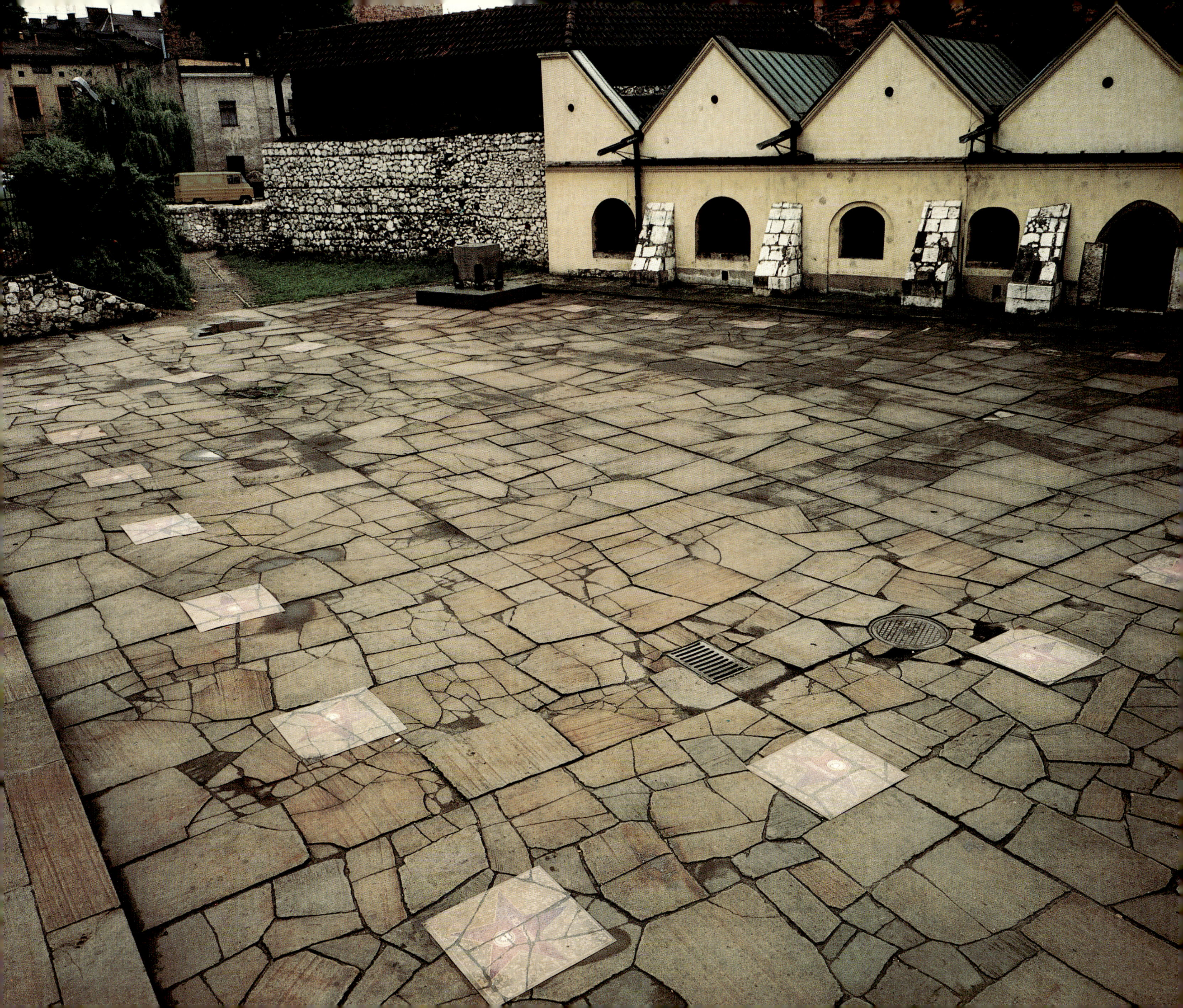

THE WRITING ON THE WALL 1991–1993

Slide projections of former Jewish residents and establishments, the *Scheunenviertel* neighborhood, Berlin, Germany

The Writing on the Wall project was realized in Berlin's former Jewish quarter, the *Scheunenviertel*, located in the Eastern part of the city, close to the Alexanderplatz.
At the heart of Berlin, the *Scheunenviertel* was a center for eastern European Jewish immigrants from the turn of the century. The few historical photographs which remained after the Holocaust reflect the world of the Jewish working class rather than that of the more affluent and assimilated German Jews who lived mostly in the Western part of the city. For this project, portions of pre-war photographs of Jewish streets were slide projected onto the same or nearby addresses today, 60 years later. The projections were visible to street traffic, neighborhood residents and passersby. By using slide projection on location, fragments of the past were introduced into the visual field of the present. Thus parts of long destroyed Jewish community life were visually simulated, momentarily recreated. As with all of his projects, Shimon Attie photographically documented the installations, creating images in which two slices of time are captured in one frame.
The *Scheunenviertel* today is a neighborhood undergoing rapid gentrification. After the fall of the Berlin Wall, the *Scheunenviertel* became the new chic quarter and frontier for many West Berliners. As a result, the neighborhood has seen a huge influx of new residents (and capital) formerly from the West.
In the very few years that have passed since Shimon Attie realized *The Writing on the Wall*, many of the houses and buildings used in the project have become unrecognizable. Most have been entirely renovated, from the inside out. Others have been transformed into fashionable and trendy bars and restaurants.
The "re-making" of the *Scheunenviertel* affects both Jewish as well as post-war East German collective memory and identity, as the last physical evidence of these histories is now disappearing as well.
The Writing on the Wall was realized over the course of approximately 1 year.

95 Joachimstraße 11a: *Former Jewish-owned bird shop and café with patrons, 1931–33, 1992*

97 Joachimstraße 11a: *Former Jewish café with patrons, 1933, 1992*

99 Joachimstraße 2: *Former Jewish resident, ca. 1930, 1992*

101 Almstadtstraße 43 (formerly Grenadierstraße 7): *Former Hebrew bookstore, 1930, 1992*

103 Almstadtstraße 5 (formerly Grenadierstraße 24): *Former Jewish resident and hat shop, ca. 1930, 1993*

105 Linienstraße 137: *Police raid on former Jewish residents, 1920, 1992*

107 Joachimstraße 20: *Former Jewish resident, theatre, and Torah reading room, 1929–31, 1992*

109 Steinstraße 21: *Former Jewish-owned pigeon shop, 1931, 1993*

111 Almstadtstraße (formerly Grenadierstraße)/ corner Schendelgasse: *Former religious book salesman, 1930, 1992*

113 Steinstraße 22: *Former Jewish residents,1932, 1993*

115 Mulackstraße 37: *Former Jewish residents, ca. 1932, 1992*

117 Mulackstraße 37: *Former kosher butcher shop and laundry, 1930, 1992*

119 Joachimstraße/corner Auguststraße: *Former Jewish resident, 1931, 1992*

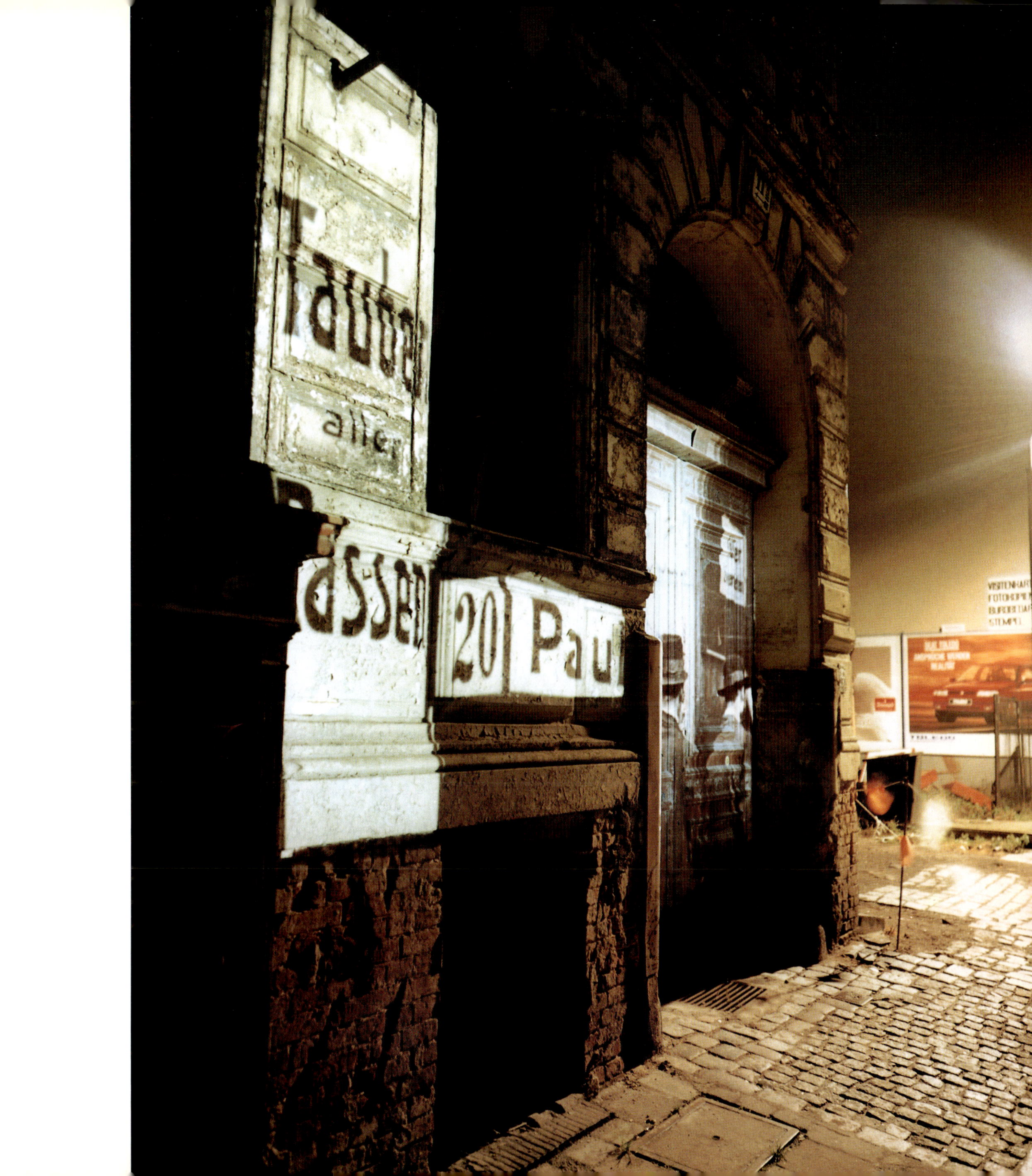
aller
20
Pau

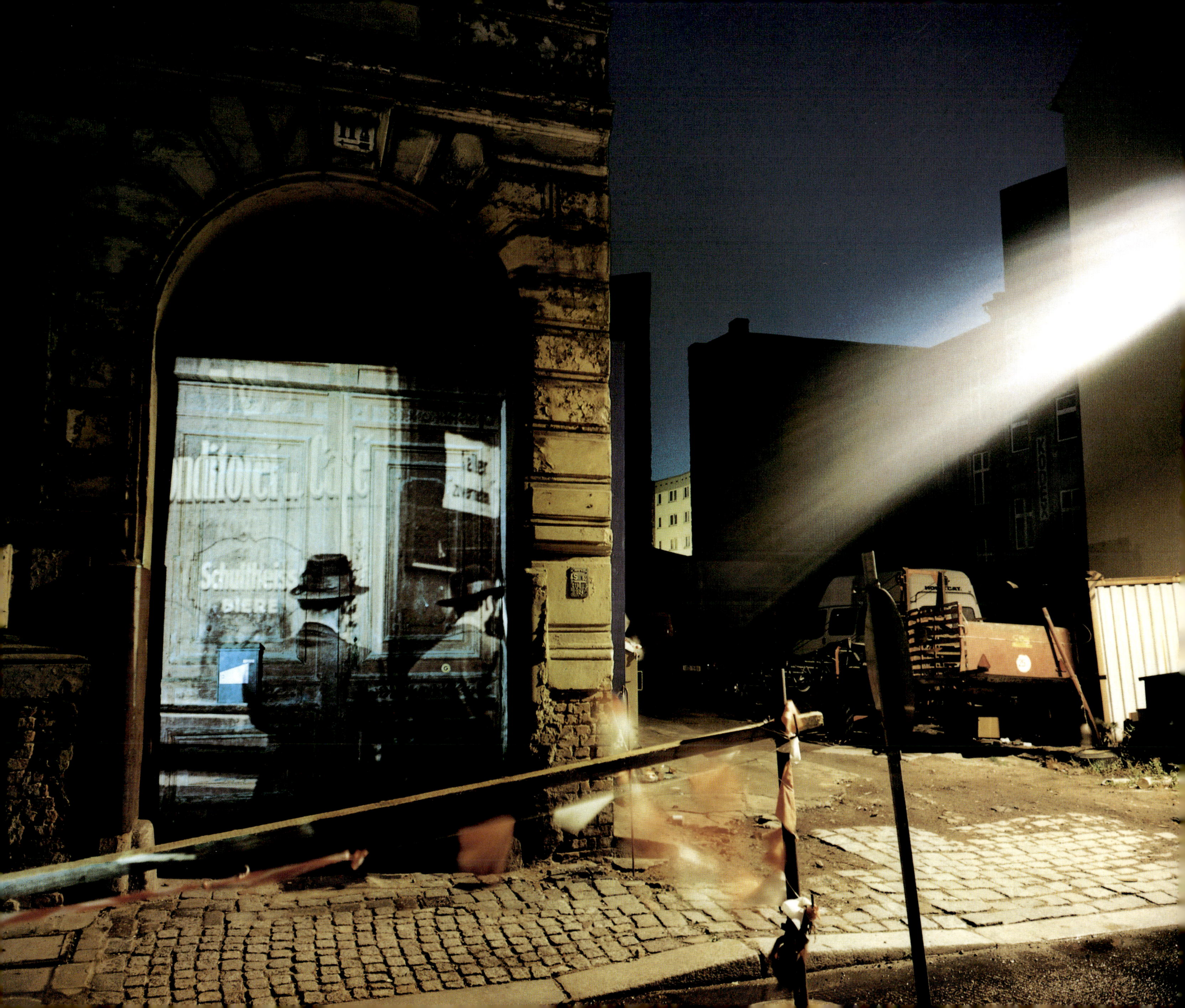
onditorei u. Café
Schultheiss
BIERE

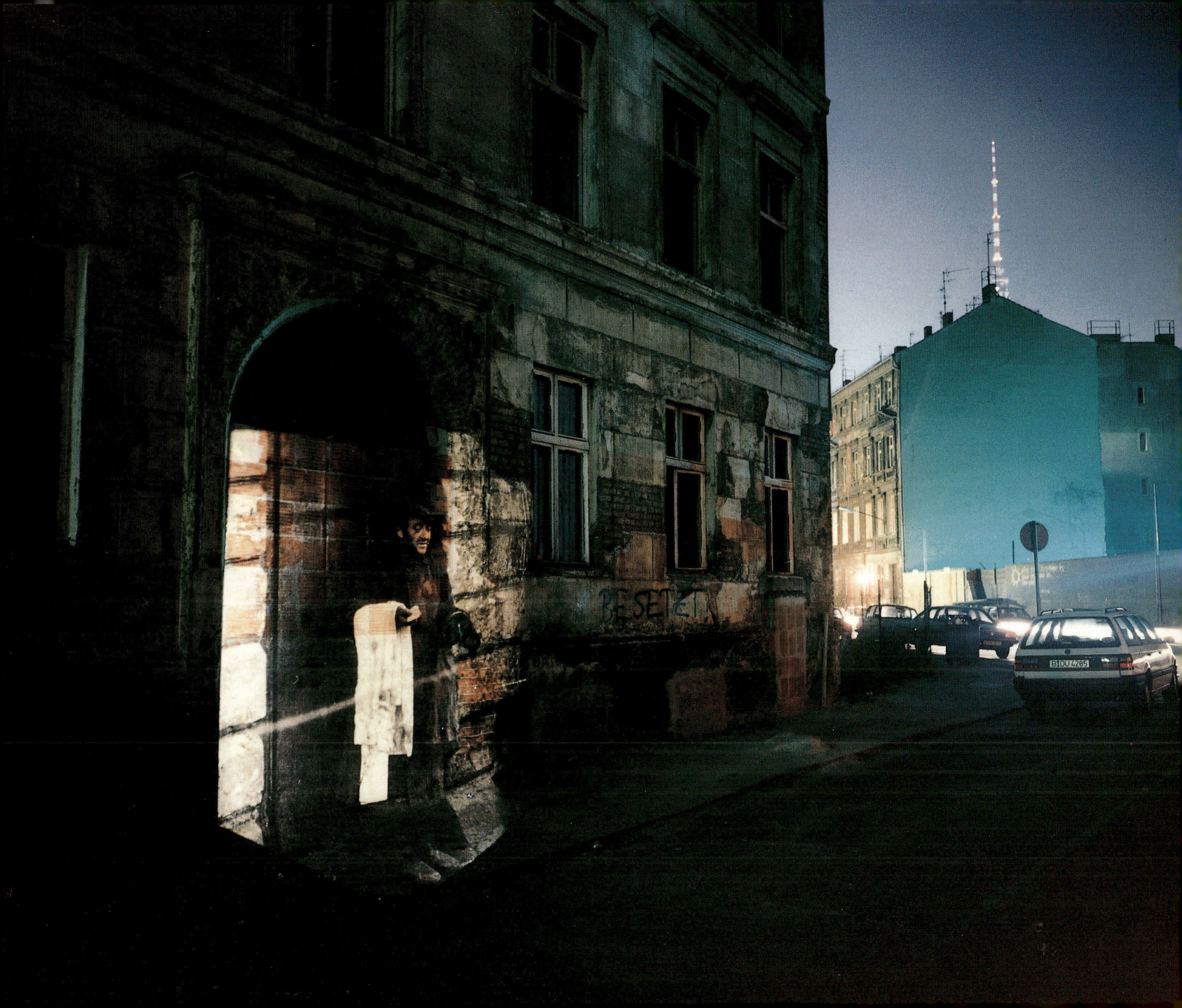
B DU 4285

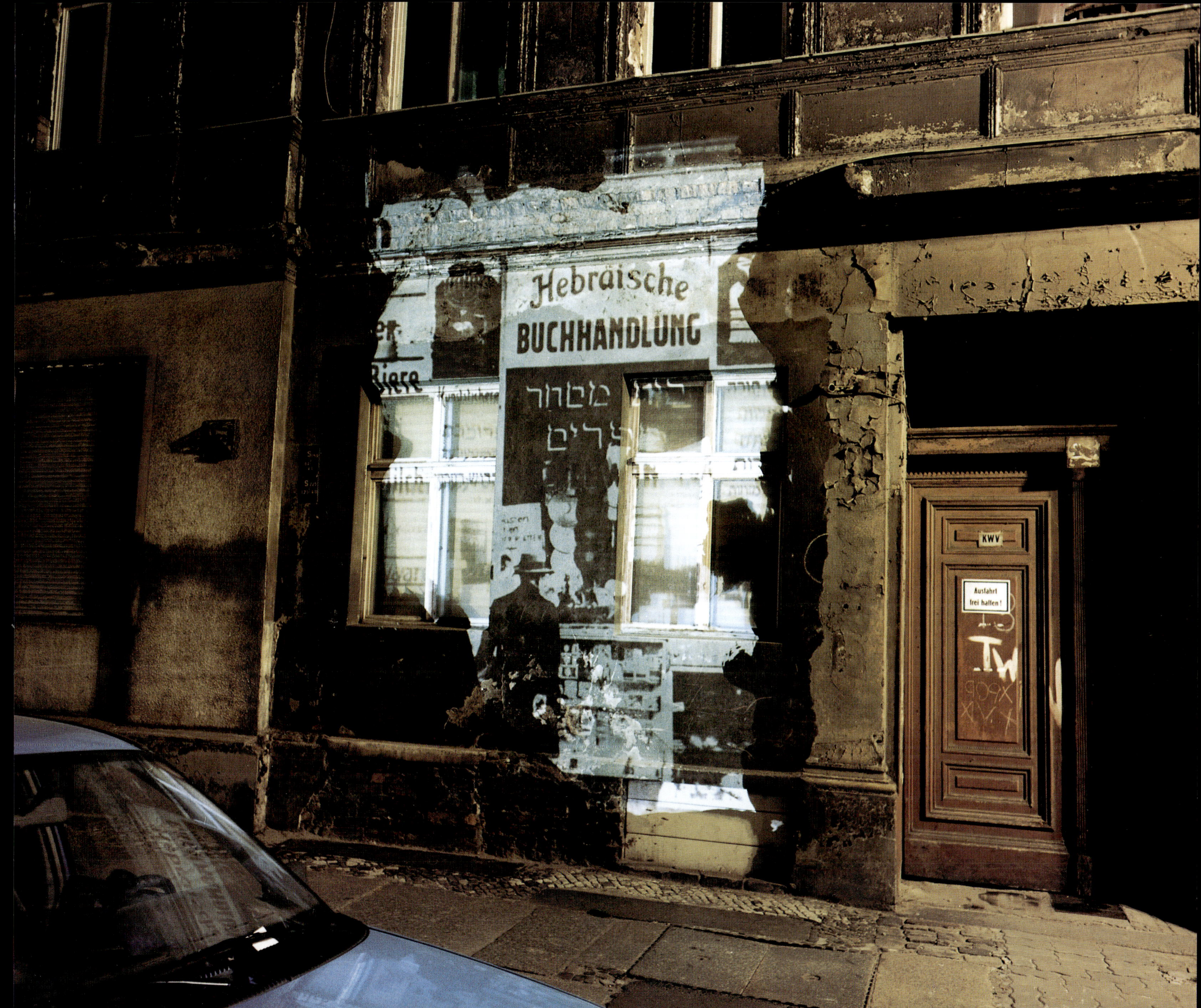
Hebräische
BUCHHANDLUNG
KWV
Ausfahrt
frei halten!

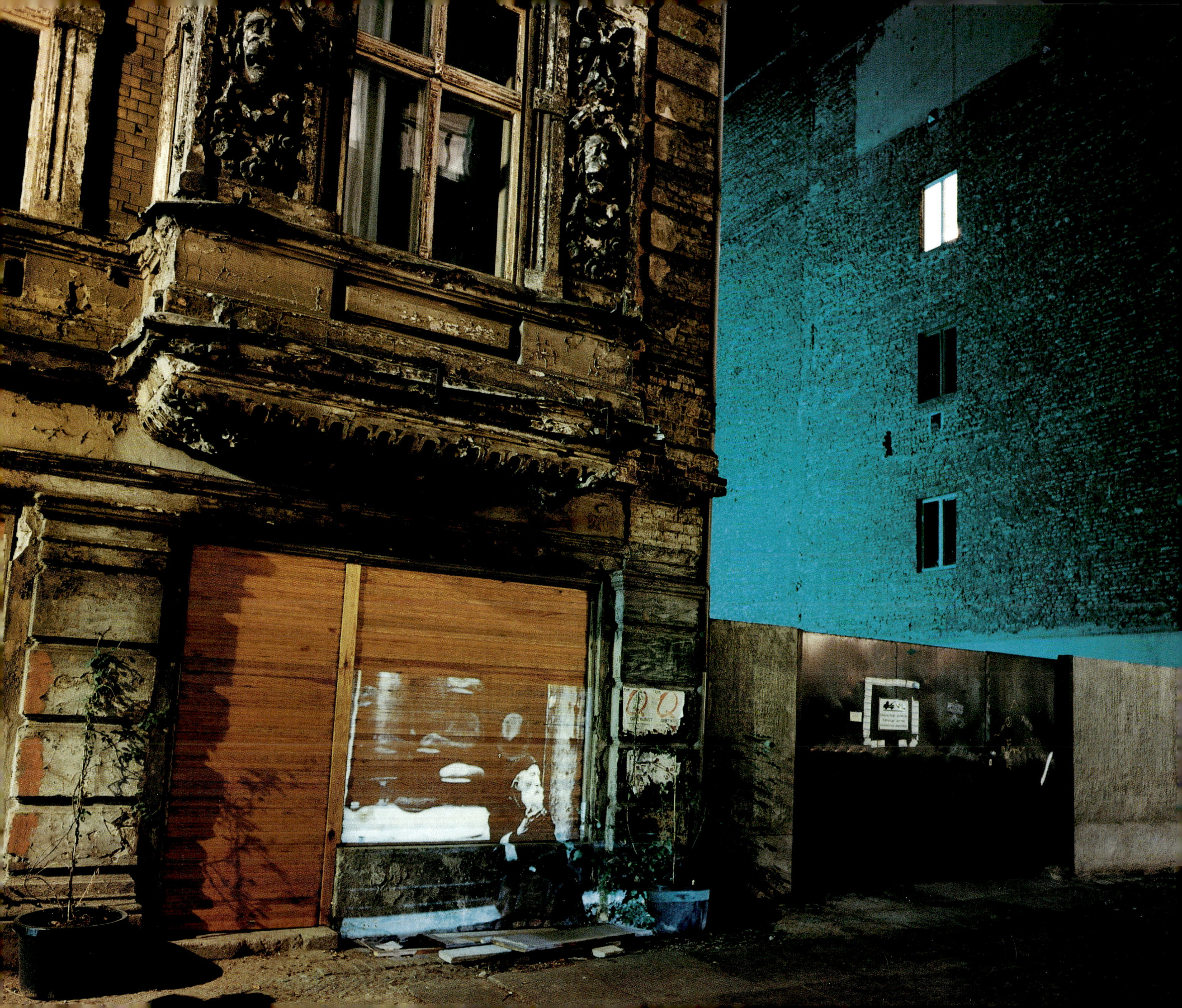

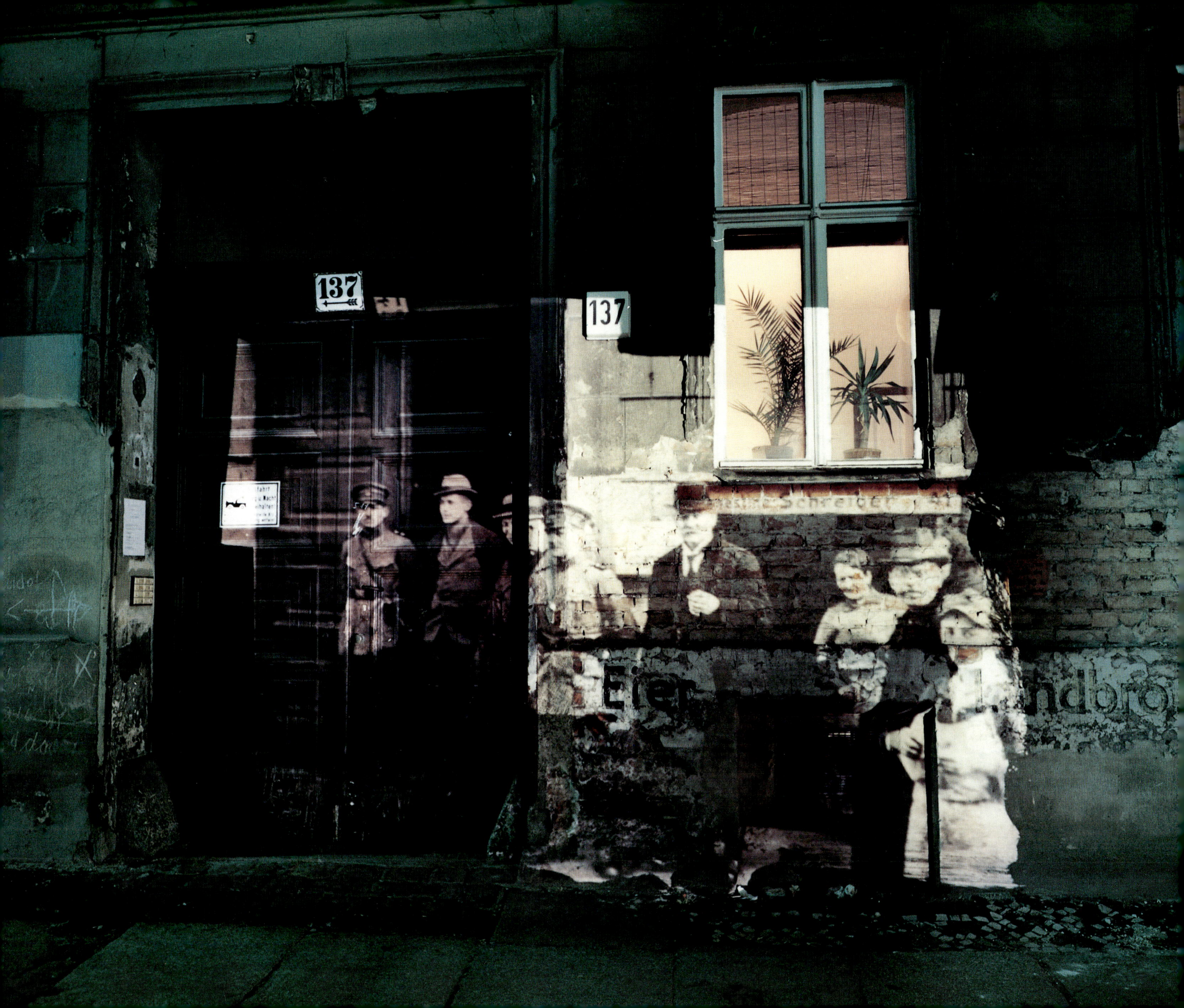
137
137
Eier

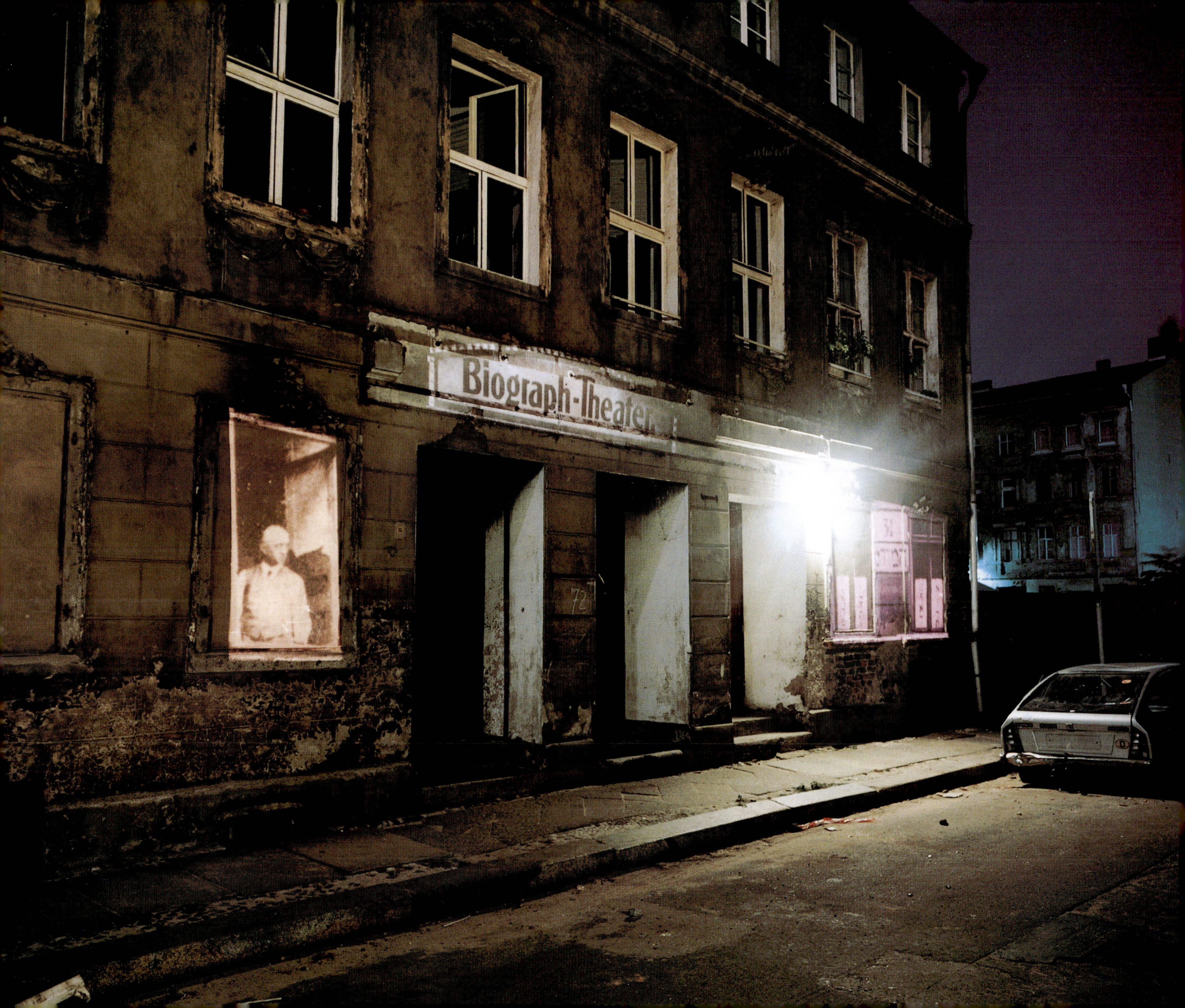
Biograph-Theater

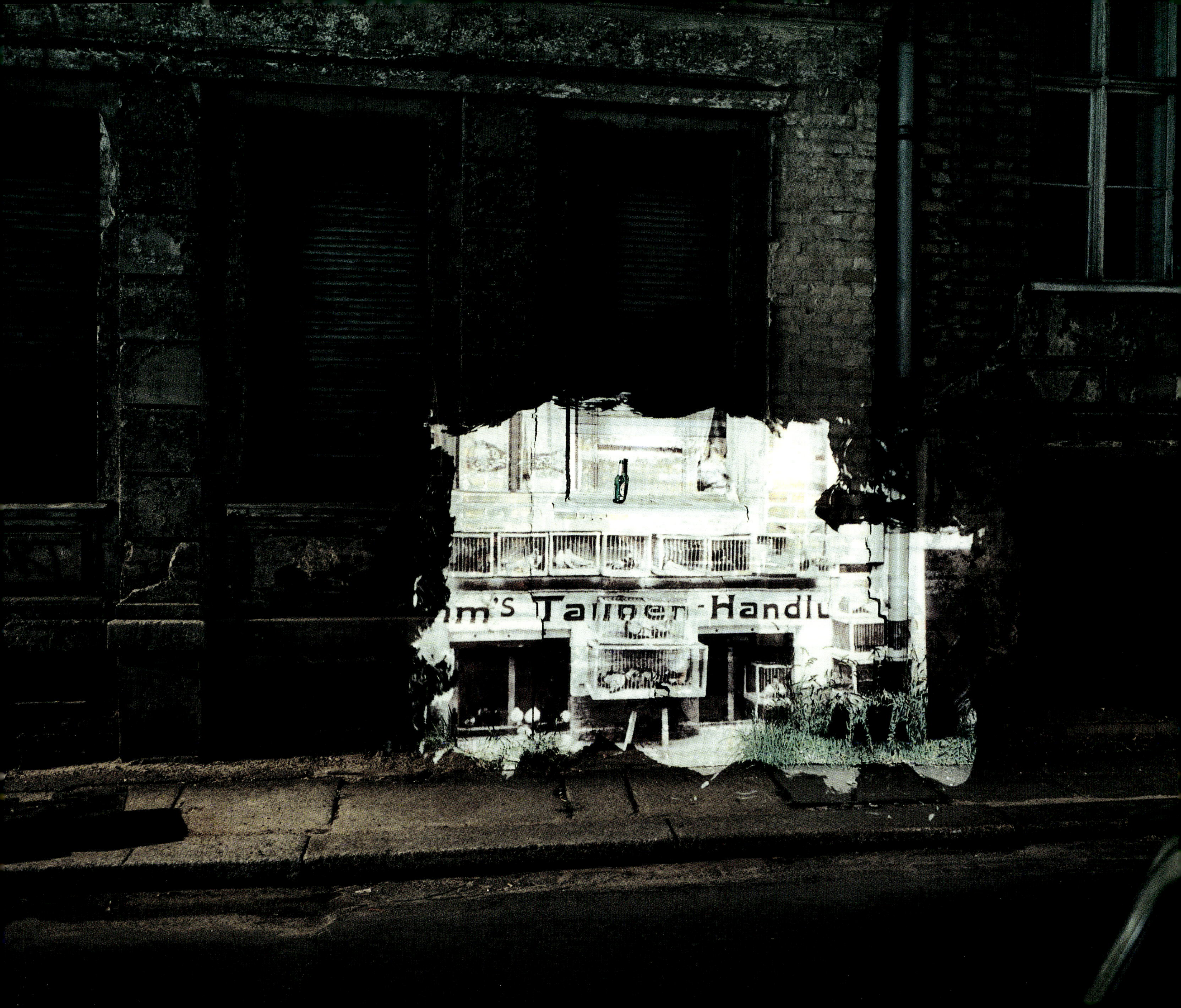

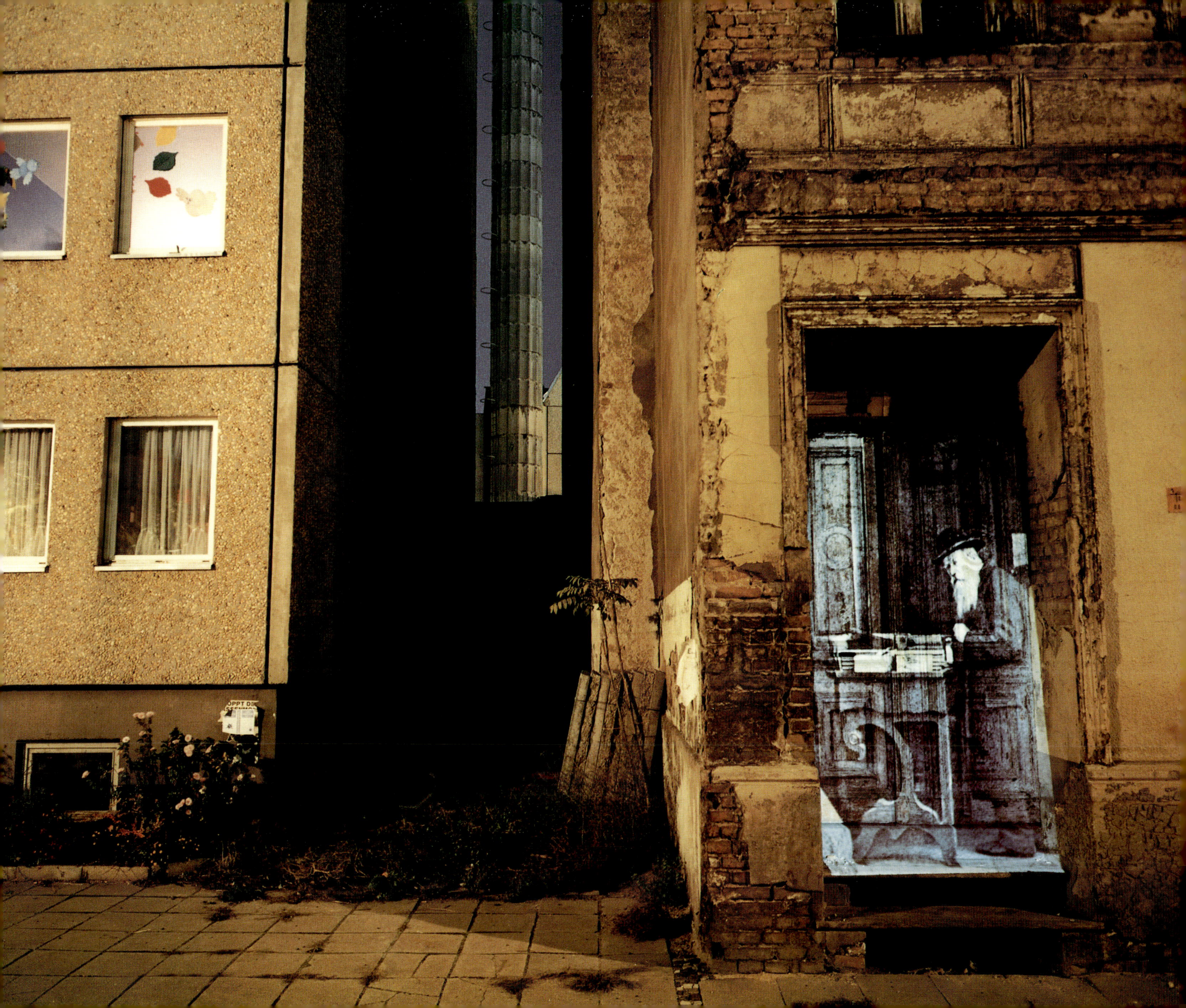

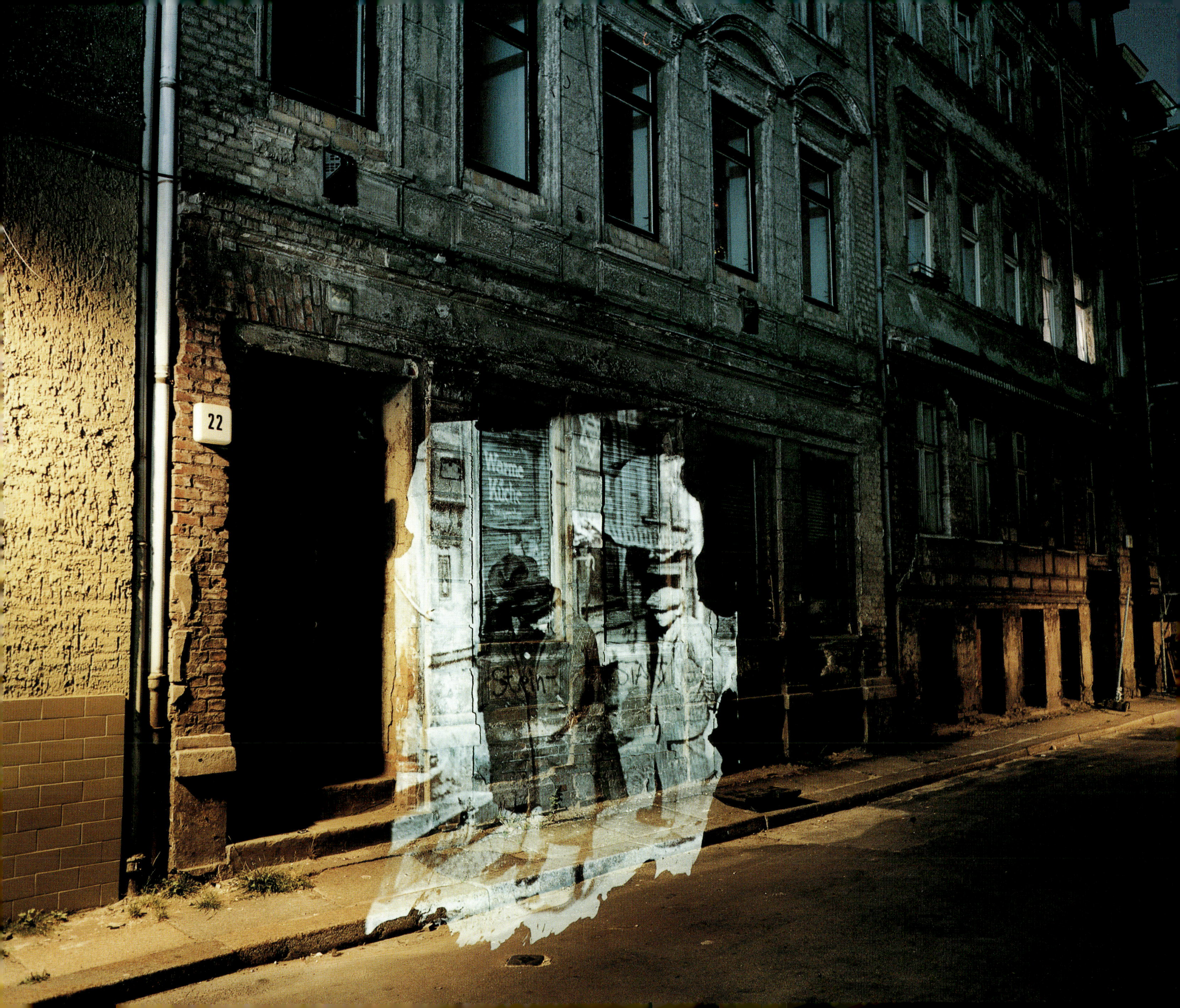
22
Warme
Küche

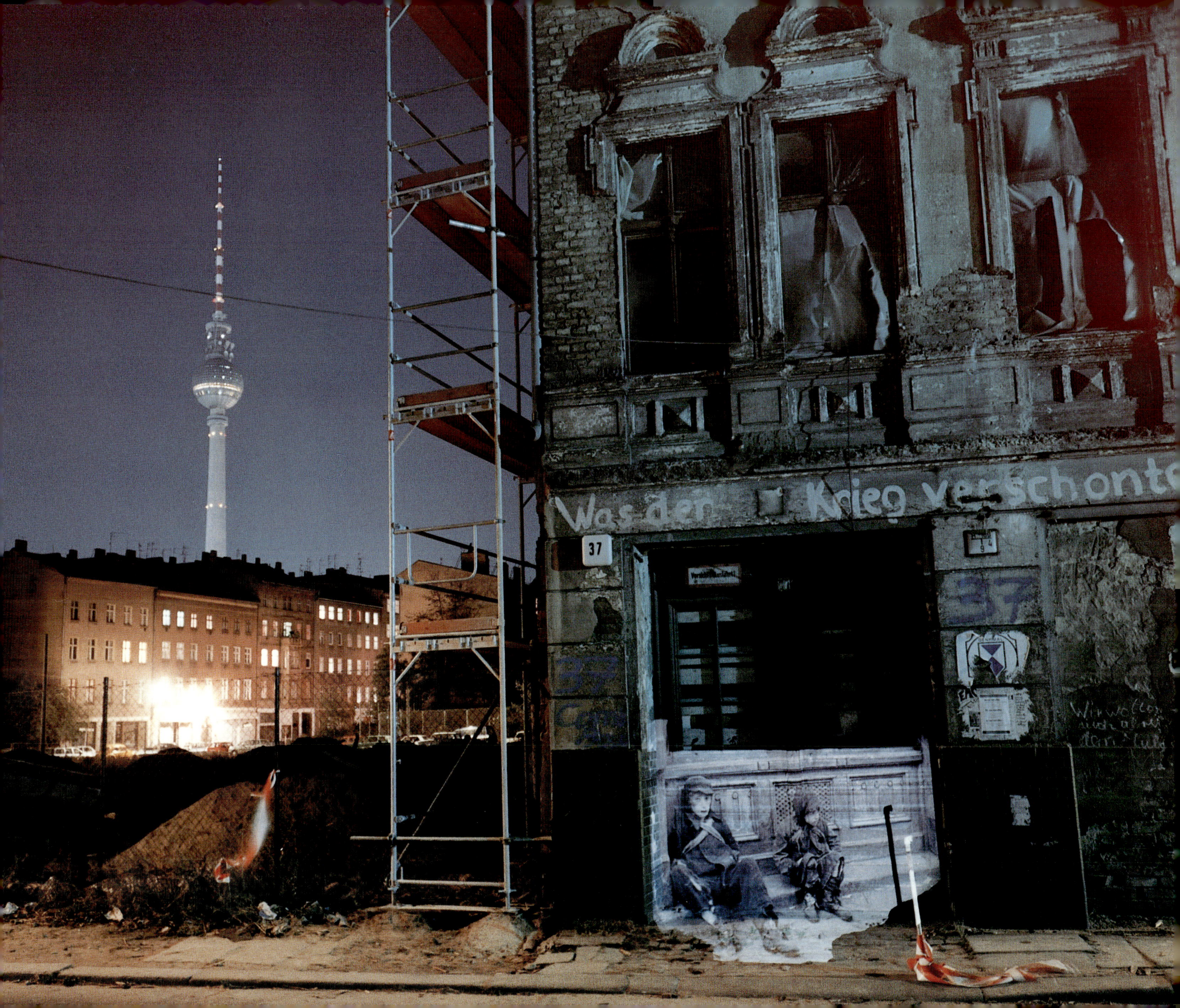
Was den Krieg verschonte
37

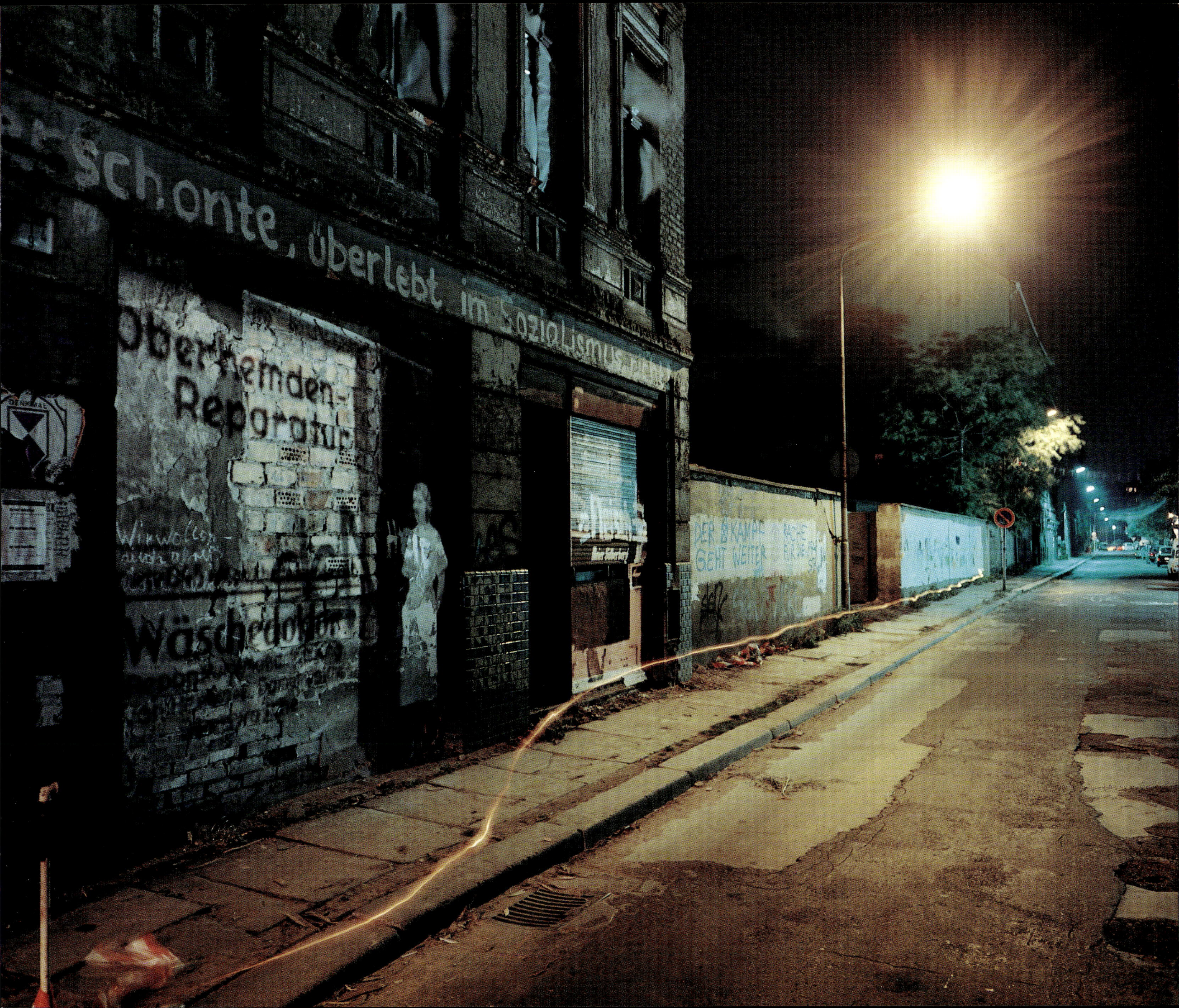
schonte, überlebt im Sozialismus
Oberhemden-
Reparatur
Wäschedoktor
DER KAMPF
GEHT WEITER

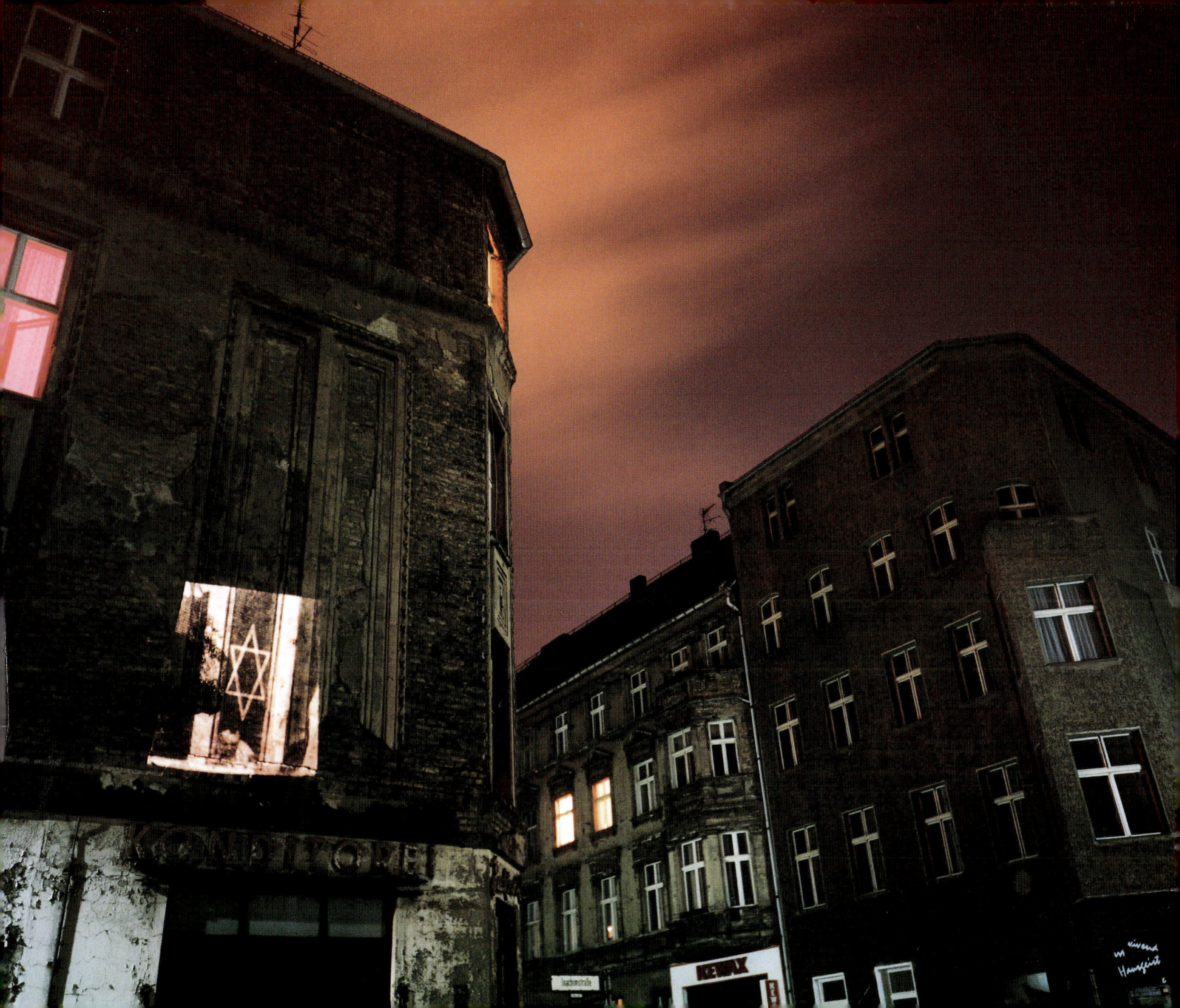

16041 ✓

ABOUT THE ARTIST

Shimon Attie was born in Los Angeles, California in 1957. He grew up in the Los Angeles area and spent two years in Israel as a teenager. Upon returning to the United States, he moved to San Francisco in order to pursue his studies. He first studied psychology at the University of California at Berkeley and at Antioch University, where he received a Bachelor of Arts degree and Master of Arts degree, respectively.

Attie began taking photographs and producing art projects in 1982. From the beginning, much of his work has combined elements of photography with on-location installation. He later received a Master of Fine Arts degree with an emphasis in art and photography from San Francisco State University. Shortly thereafter, in 1991, he moved to Europe in order to work on Sites Unseen.

His work is in the permanent collection of many major museums, and has been exhibited widely across the United States and Europe, including at the Museum of Modern Art in New York.

Boston's Institute of Contemporary Art (ICA) is currently organizing a travelling mid-career retrospective exhibition of Attie's work for the Fall of 1999.

Attie has received four year-long visual artist fellowships, including from the National Endowment for the Arts in the United States and Kunstfonds in Germany. In addition, he has been awarded major project commissions from a number of prestigious sources, including the European Community in Brussels, the Danish Ministries of Culture and Interior, and the Mondriaan Foundation in the Netherlands.

Shimon Attie currently divides his time between New York and San Francisco, and is represented by Jack Shainman Gallery in New York City, Robert Koch Gallery in San Francisco, and Galerie Claude Samuel in Paris.